PRAY LIKE
JESUS

Lessons from the Gospel of Luke

JEFF BELCHER

LifeWay Press® Nashville, Tennessee

Student Ministry Publishing

Ben Trueblood
Director, Student Ministry

John Paul Basham
*Manager, Student
Ministry Publishing*

Karen Daniel
Editorial Team Leader

Andy McLean
Content Editor

Jennifer Siao
Production Editor

Amy Lyon
Graphic Designer

ISBN: 978-1-4627-9220-7
Item Number: 005801310

Dewey Decimal Classification Number: 248.3
Subject Heading: Christian Experience / Worship and Prayer

Printed in the United States of America.

Student Ministry Publishing
LifeWay Resources
One LifeWay Plaza
Nashville, TN 37234

We believe that the Bible has God for its author; salvation for its end; and truth, without any mixture of error, for its matter and that all Scripture is totally true and trustworthy. To review LifeWay's doctrinal guideline, please visit www.lifeway.com/doctrinalguideline.

Unless otherwise noted, all Scripture quotations are taken from the Christian Standard Bible®, Copyright ©2017 by Holman Bible Publishers. Used by permission. Christian Standard Bible® and CSB® are federally registered trademarks of Holman Bible Publishers.

TABLE OF CONTENTS

INTRO

Before Jesus left the earth He passed on to His disciples the responsibility of continuing His mission, and shortly after He ascended to heaven, the Holy Spirit came upon Jesus' followers to empower them to live out His calling in their lives.

To be a Christian is to choose a lifestyle that looks like Jesus in every way. We're to follow Jesus in the ways we demonstrate love and compassion to others. We're to live like Him in pursuing God with unwavering devotion. We're to follow Christ in setting aside our own desires in order to fulfill the Father's will. And we're to imitate Jesus in pursuing a lifestyle of continual prayer.

Jesus, while He was on earth, prayed in a much different way than the average Christian does today. In this study on prayer, we're going to look closely at the ways Jesus prayed in the accounts found in Luke's Gospel. Luke wrote to reveal Jesus in His humanity. Even though Jesus is fully God, He's also fully man and, while He was on earth, He faced the same kinds of struggles you and I face today. The difference is, He never even once gave into temptation. By paying attention to the prayer life of Jesus—when He prayed, how He prayed, why He prayed—we'll learn a few things about ways we can overcome the weaknesses of our human condition and equip ourselves to live more fully by the Spirit and to please God.

ABOUT THE AUTHOR

JEFF BELCHER has been involved in ministry since 1997, including time spent traveling in a worship band and serving as both a student minister and worship pastor within the local church. Jeff currently serves as a church planter with the North American Mission Board and is working to establish Church of the Harbor in Baltimore, MD. He holds a bachelor's in music from the University of Alabama and received his master's in counseling from Liberty University. Jeff also works with LifeWay as an editor for *Bible Studies for Life: Students*. Jeff and his wife, Kelly, live in Baltimore with their six kids and German Shepherd. They enjoy live music and theater, time in the outdoors, good Southern food, and cheering on the Crimson Tide. No matter the expression, Jeff's passion has always been the same— to share the gospel with anyone who will listen and to help people grow in their devotion to Jesus.

This study contains eight weekly group sessions. Each group session is designed to be approximately one hour, with about 10 minutes of video teaching and 50 minutes of group interaction/discussion.

Each session consists of an engage/introduction section, a group discussion guide, an application section, and five days of personal devotions. There is also a leader guide at the back of this study with helpful tips for leaders as they prepare to lead the main group time. As you finish each group session, encourage students to complete the personal devotions before your next meeting.

Engage

Every session contains an introduction to that week's session material, allowing for a natural transition into the biblical content for that week.

Watch

Each session has a corresponding video to help explain the biblical content. Allow students to write down and notes and questions that may arise from the video and discuss them together before moving to the Group Discussion section.

Group Discussion

After watching the video, continue the study by moving to the group discussion and working through the content provided there. The content provided in this section will expand on what was introduced in the video, offering greater clarity into the meaning of the passages under consideration.

Prayer in Real Life

Following the group discussion is the application section, entitled Prayer in Real Life. As a group, work through the content provided here before closing your group time in prayer.

Devotions

Five personal devotions are provided for each session to take individuals deeper into Scripture and to supplement the content introduced in the group study. With biblical teaching and questions of personal application, these sections challenge students to grow in their understanding of God's Word and to respond in faith.

Session 1
AT HIS BAPTISM

Focal Passage // Luke 3:21-22

Memory Verse // Ephesians 6:18

Pray at all times in the Spirit with every prayer and request, and stay alert with all perseverance and intercession for all the saints.

Weekly Reading // Luke 1:1–4:13

We've all had "big days."

- You've anticipated for years getting your driver's license, but first you have to pass the driving test—which is tomorrow!

- You've dreamed for years of the freedoms associated with going to college, and you'll be heading out of town next week—which is both exhilarating and terrifying!

Sometimes we take these big days head-on, and other times we'd rather hide under the covers and wait for time to pass us by. Sure, they can be exciting, but there's often a lot of pressure. We all know that change and growth can be difficult. Either way, whereas the large majority of our lives consists of routine, ordinary days, we all experience monumental moments that have a profound effect on the future and direction of all the days that follow.

Describe a "big day" you've experienced. What was the occasion? What made it more significant than any other day?

In Luke 2, we read that "Jesus increased in wisdom and stature, and in favor with God and with people" (Luke 2:52). Joseph, Jesus' earthly father, was a carpenter, and Jesus had followed in His father's footsteps (Matt. 13:55; Mark 6:3).

Though it may be hard to imagine considering Jesus is God, He spent day after day learning skills from His dad and developing the techniques and muscle memory necessary to build with excellence. Most of His days were ordinarily routine—He ate His vegetables and did His work—and He grew up like any young man. Life was simple and beautiful. Undoubtedly, however, there were days when Jesus experienced things that were especially meaningful, and all the days that followed were different because of these experiences. Maybe it was the day He figured out how to drive a nail with a one-hammer stroke, or He finally got a thumbs-up from His dad concerning a particular style of table which had given Him trouble.

When Jesus began His public ministry, He experienced one of the most monumental days of His life. He'd always lived in obedience to God, but the challenges that lay ahead were particularly difficult, and Jesus' baptism was huge. It was the day everything changed.

Watch this session's video, and then continue to the group discussion section using the content provided.

THE SPIRIT'S POWER

As a student, you likely live with your parents or someone else who has responsibility for you, and they provide the things you need to live, learn, and grow. They know your favorite foods, the brand of jeans you prefer, and that you need a new pair of soccer shoes. Why? Because the last time your mom made tacos, you ate eleven, and because you've complained about the hole in your cleats for the past three weeks. Your parents or guardians are able to meet your needs (and likely give you many things you want) because they know you from communicating with you.

How would you describe your communication with your parents or guardians?

In your own words, how would you define prayer?

John the Baptist taught that baptism was a sign of repentance (Matt. 3:11), and when Jesus came to John to be baptized, initially John refused. After all, Jesus didn't need to repent of anything. However, Jesus insisted, John relented, and as Jesus was picturing for all those who would look upon His baptism—both in person and through the pages of Scripture— the death and resurrection He would soon experience, He was also praying.

Prayer was very important in Jewish culture, and children were taught from a young age to pray. Considering Mary and Joseph were faithful Jews, they undoubtedly taught Jesus to pray. Further, Jesus was God's Son, and we can be confident He lived continually in a close relationship with His heavenly Father as He grew in favor with Him. Prayer was naturally a part of Jesus' experience; however, He knew His baptism signified a moment of dramatic change in His life. Thirty years was the customary age for entering into the office of prophet, priest, or king, and Jesus would take the colossal step from a carpenter's lifestyle to that of sacrificial ministry, and He would serve God's people in a way none other ever could.

Because Jesus knew what the future held and the plan His Father had for Him, He recognized that, as a man, He needed help from above:
- To remain closely connected with the Father
- To remain continually dependent upon the Spirit for strength and guidance

So on this monumental occasion, He prayed. And in that moment, Jesus' prayer became a catalyst for something supernatural to occur in His life. The heavens were literally torn open and the Spirit descended upon Jesus in the form of a dove. In a sense, Jesus was being anointed as the Prophet who would bring God's final and best message to all people. He was being set apart as the great High Priest who would make a way for people to come into God's presence. He was being empowered to establish God's kingdom on earth, over which He would reign as King.

In order to accomplish the Father's plan for His life, because Jesus had given up certain divine privileges when He came to earth, He knew that He would need to live in continual connection with and dependence upon the Father and the Spirit. So He prayed—and the Spirit came upon Him.

How do you rely on the Holy Spirit in your day-to-day pursuit of God?

THE FATHER'S APPROVAL

Teenagers are naturally better at some things than others, and the fact that we're all different makes the world a richer place. You may be exceptional in academics, perhaps you're an outstanding athlete, or maybe you excel in the arts. Whatever the case, to grow in any of these areas takes hard work, patience, and even sacrifice. But it's all worth it. One reason is because there are likely few things that make your parents prouder than seeing you shine as you live in your element—the things you were created to do. How do you feel when you parents (or other people of authority in your life) express their pleasure in you?

There are basically two types of prayers: 1) prayer for the purpose of devotion, and 2) prayer for the purpose of supplication. This second type is when we make requests of God, when we depend on Him and ask Him for things only He can provide. However, sometimes it's easy to fall into the habit of asking God to give us things that we may not necessarily need, or even things that aren't in line with His will.

At Jesus' baptism, He didn't pray to ask God for anything. Rather, He prayed as a matter of devotion and relationship with the Father. He loved His Father so much that, as a matter of the heart, Jesus naturally lived in continual communication with Him. As Jesus prayed, not only did the sky split and the Holy Spirit come down from heaven, but the very voice of God sounded from the heavens—"You are my beloved Son; with you I am well-pleased" (Mark 1:11).

For the thirty years leading up to Jesus' baptism, everything Jesus had done—including the things He said and thought—pleased the Father. He'd obeyed perfectly, He'd been perfectly grateful, and worked diligently at everything (imagine being Jesus' brother ... just saying), and Jesus' love for and devotion to the Father was central to this. At Jesus' baptism, God was certainly pleased that Jesus was submitting to the Father's will and pursuing the purposes that lay before Him. But the words from heaven signified much more than that. God was pleased with Jesus in the fullest sense.

THE SON'S PREPARATION

The world is all around us. That seems absurdly obvious, right? Here's what I mean: in the stories your friends tell at school, the TV shows you veg out to, the music that flows into your ears (and your heart), you're surrounded by worldly values. And these values are saturated with temptations that would draw you away from God and toward ruin.

What temptations do you face that would, if you gave in, draw you away from God and bring harm to your life?

One of the big purposes of Jesus' coming to earth was that He would become our High Priest. This means He left heaven, took on the form of a man, and became subject to our weaknesses and temptations so that He could personally relate to us in our struggles. Jesus' baptism was a turning point in His life which involved His leaving carpentry and launching into ministry, and crossing this threshold involved the temptation He would experience in the desert (Luke 4:1-13). The Holy Spirit, who had just descended upon Jesus like a peaceful dove, then cast Him violently (that's the literal meaning of "led" in Luke 4:1) away from the comfort and safety of like-minded people and into the desert all alone.

The Scriptural perspective on the desert is this—it's a place where fugitives and bandits hide out, where wild beasts are free to roam and execute violence against weaker creatures, and where, in general, bad things happen. In a word, danger! Further, the desert is a picture of the lack of God's blessing—it's a barren place due to lack of rain, and not even vegetation grows there. In the desert, Jesus was exposed and vulnerable, even tempted by the devil himself, and in all the ways we are tempted every day:

- Jesus had fasted forty days, and He was hungry, so Satan tempted Him by appealing to His fleshly desires, specifically food.

- Because Jesus was seeking followers, the devil said to Him essentially, "Throw yourself from the temple. God won't let you be hurt and all the people will know who you are."

- Jesus knew that the cross lay ahead of Him, and the devil tried to get Jesus to take the easy way out by basically saying—"Just worship me and I'll give you the world—after all, it's mine to give."

On a certain level, these seem like pretty good options, at least from a worldly perspective. That's why it's tempting. But, even though giving in would have been much easier, Jesus didn't come to earth to live a comfortable and convenient life. His highest priority was to please the Father and accomplish His purposes.

Jesus' baptism prayer helped strengthen Him for the tests in the desert, and Jesus' living in continual prayer helped Him remain strong to pass every test along the way.

1. The Spirit's Power

Jesus is literally God in the flesh. He is fully divine, yet somehow He is also human in every way. Jesus knew that in order to successfully accomplish the Father's purposes, He'd need to depend on the Holy Spirit. If Jesus needed to pray, how much more do we?

What weaknesses are you discovering in your life? Maybe even things you once thought were no issue at all?

How have you seen the Holy Spirit help you live well in a way you couldn't have without Him?

2. The Father's Approval

The Father expressed His perfect approval in His Son. God created us with certain desires that point to bigger spiritual realities, and these words—with you I'm well-pleased—are words we all long to hear from our parents, at least on some level. Ultimately, we all want to hear this from God, but the truth of the matter is, we can never be good enough to please Him. However, when we live by faith in His Son, God is pleased with us in Jesus.

What are some areas of your life you think God would be pleased with? What may you need to change?

3. The Son's Preparation

At His baptism, Jesus knew that He would soon be tempted in the desert, so He prayed as an act of preparation for what He would soon face. We can be sure that, pretty much every day, we too will face temptations from the world.

What sorts of temptations do you think you may face in the near future?

What are you doing, day by day, to prepare to live successfully through those trials?

PRAY LIKE JESUS

Take a few minutes now and pray:
- That the Spirit would powerfully involve Himself in your life
- That the Father would help you live day by day, moment by moment in ways that are pleasing to Him
- That you would be, through your devotional life, prepared to overcome temptation and live in obedience to the Father

"This is my servant; I strengthen him, this is my chosen one; I delight in him. I have put my Spirit on him; he will bring justice to the nations. He will not cry out or shout or make his voice heard in the streets. He will not break a bruised reed, and he will not put out a smoldering wick; he will faithfully bring justice. He will not grow weak or be discouraged until he has established justice on earth. The coasts and islands will wait for his instruction." **ISAIAH 42:1-4**

Let's be honest: school can be a tough place. You may have to catch the bus while it's still dark outside, class can be insanely boring, there's all the homework—and this is the easy stuff. There are bullies and mean girls, impossibly difficult questions about future and purpose, and on and on. Sometimes life can be painful and unfair.

For generations, God's people had anticipated the coming of the Messiah. He would rescue them from oppression and slavery. He would, as Isaiah puts it, "bring justice to the nations" (v. 1). This means all the world's wrongs would be made right, and everyone would get what's coming to them. From Israel's perspective, the bad guys would pay, and the good guys would, of course, receive the honor and blessing they rightly deserved— they were God's chosen, after all (hint: Only Jesus is good, and we're all bad guys who deserve God's punishment. Faith in Jesus allows us to receive God's favor). They expected a great political leader, or maybe a mighty warrior—basically a man's man who didn't need anything from anyone. The Messiah would be a conqueror!

Isaiah, 700 years before Jesus was born, wrote about God's coming Messiah. He wouldn't be bold and brash, but would have a generally quiet and submissive demeanor—He would be a servant. He wouldn't work the ways the politically elite normally do it, campaigning and seeking favors from those with power—He would comfort the hurting and love the unlovable. Contrary to the world's ways, the Messiah would bring perfect justice.

When Jesus came to earth, He didn't come as a warrior fighting on behalf of God's people —at least not the way the people expected. Instead, Jesus humbled Himself and came as a servant. In fact, He set aside particular powers and privileges associated with being God in order to experience human weakness. This meant He had to rely on the Spirit to fulfill God's purposes for His chosen One.

When Jesus prayed at His baptism, we don't know exactly what He prayed. We do know, however, that in that moment, the heavens opened and the Spirit came upon Him. God had a big plan for Jesus—He would bring perfect justice to the world. This was a monumental task, and Jesus the man, from that moment forward, had the Spirit helping Him to live in obedience, even through the monstrous temptations He'd face over the next three years.

We, too, if we are part of God's family, have the Holy Spirit in our lives. If Jesus (who is God) needed to pray in order to live by the Spirit's power, how much more do we? Let's make today the momentous occasion when we commit to living by prayer.

In practical terms, describe what it looks like to live in prayerful reliance on the Spirit versus living by our own strength.

ON MY OWN

- Example: When a friend annoys me, though I try hard not to, I tend to snap at them.

-

-

BY THE SPIRIT

- Example: When a friend annoys me, I pray and remind myself to see them as God does, and I treat them kindly.

-

-

What is God calling you to change about your prayer life? Commit to two things:

PRAY WITH JESUS

Father, I face temptations and difficulties every day, and I know it's impossible for me to live the way You want me to own my own. Please help me to continually rely on the Spirit's power so that Your purposes can be accomplished in my life.

JOURNAL YOUR OWN PRAYER:

*"I will declare the L*ORD*'s decree. He said to me, 'You are my Son; today I have become your Father. Ask of me, and I will make the nations your inheritance and the ends of the earth your possession. You will break them with an iron scepter; you will shatter them like pottery.'"*
PSALM 2:7-9

Certain privileges are earned. The first chair trumpet player worked hard and for many, many hours to earn that position. The quarterback earned the job by spending time in the weight room, and watching film, and throwing many passes. However, the trumpeter and quarterback were more than likely born with a certain level of talent others might not have. Yes, many privileges are attained by hard work, but some advantages we're simply born with. What privilege do you enjoy that you've worked for? What's one you were born into?

When people rebelled against God and brought the curse upon creation, God gave, in a certain sense, authority over the world to the kingdom of darkness (1 John 5:19; Luke 4:6). No longer would God reign in the lives of all people—instead, we would have the choice to follow Satan in rebellion against the Creator, or we could submit in obedience to the will of God. However, Satan's power is limited, and God will ultimately accomplish His will according to His sovereign power. All along, God had a plan to bring restoration to the brokenness we've caused by our sin, and ultimately, He'll return rule over creation to its rightful place.

Jesus, the Son of God, is the one God chose (Messiah means "chosen one") to conquer sin and to reestablish God's eternal reign. When Jesus came to earth, He understood His purpose. He knew that He'd be bruised, but that through the struggle, the rejection, and the pain, He would receive as an inheritance the nations.

In 1 Samuel 16:12-13, we read of David being anointed as the future king of Israel. It would be years before his rule would be fully expressed, but from that moment, when the Spirit came powerfully upon his life, the kingdom had been given to him. In Psalm 2, David, in reflecting upon his own anointing, prophetically spoke of the reign God would bring about through the Messiah. The Lord decreed, "You are my Son; today I have become your Father" (v. 7)—Jesus is the rightful heir over all that belongs to the Father, and from the day He was anointed as the Messiah and He began the redemptive work, though His reign may not be fully expressed, creation is His.

We don't know what Jesus prayed at His baptism, however, we do know that God said to Him, "Ask of me, and I will make the nations your inheritance and the ends of the earth your possession" (v. 8). It's possible that, as He was being anointed and as the Holy Spirit was empowering Him, Jesus could have said, "Let your kingdom come! Give me the nations as an inheritance! Establish through your servant your rule and reign to the ends of the earth!"

Jesus received this privilege as a result of His being "begotten" of the Father. He is the rightful heir. As we all know, with much privilege comes much responsibility (Luke 12:48), and thankfully Jesus was humble and powerful enough to fulfill it. Today, for those who are Jesus' followers, we are "born" into the family of God as well. Though we could never achieve what Jesus has, our great blessing also comes with great responsibility. As God's sons and daughters, we are co-heirs with Jesus (Rom. 8:17), and are called to work toward seeing the kingdom made a reality on earth. We've been empowered by the Spirit. We have the privilege of praying. Commit to living in obedience to the Father, all the while praying that God would give to Christ the nations as an inheritance as He saves people, even to the ends of the earth.

What blessings from God do you see in your life? What responsibility is associated with each blessing?

What is your response to knowing you're an heir with Christ?

Jesus worked to establish God's reign on the earth. How can you work in pursuit of the same thing?

PRAY WITH JESUS

Father, thank You for considering me worthy, by Christ's sacrifice, to be called Your child. Help me, as an heir with Jesus, to live in ways that help establish Your kingdom on earth.

JOURNAL YOUR OWN PRAYER:

"When they had prayed, the place where they were assembled was shaken, and they were all filled with the Holy Spirit and began to speak the word of God boldly." **ACTS 4:31**

What we see when we look into the mirror changes from day to day. We have good hair days and bad ones. Sometimes our face is clear, and other times there are so many pimples we can't imagine leaving home. Sometimes we're proud of what we see, and other times we can see nothing but our imperfections, weaknesses, and deficiencies. What do you see about yourself that you'd like to change?

Whereas the mirror allows us to see our physical features, the truth of Scripture allows us to know ourselves emotionally, relationally, and spiritually—who we are as people. Jesus' disciples, as they followed Him, had witnessed amazing things, and they'd even been used themselves to do miracles (Matt. 10:1). However, when things got really tough, they'd turned their backs on Jesus. They were weak and imperfect, they needed Jesus, and they knew it.

Before Jesus ascended, He charged the disciples with carrying the message of the gospel to the world (Matt. 28:18-20). To this point, Jesus had preached the good news, He'd loved and served people in meaningful and miraculous ways, and He'd taught His disciples the things they needed to know. But, now that His purpose on earth had been fulfilled, it was time for Jesus to return the to the Father's side.

I can only imagine what the disciples felt. They'd loved and followed Jesus, but then, in the worst way imaginable, He'd been taken from them. They were devastated! Soon, however, they learned that their teacher, their Messiah, was alive. They were exhilarated! But the ride wasn't over yet, and soon they were witnesses to Jesus' leaving them again. As they stared into the heavens, they watched Jesus ascend and disappear into the clouds. He'd left them, again! But not before He reminded them of a promise He'd made weeks before (Acts 1:4-5; John 16:7). Jesus had told the disciples that He would leave, and even though it may have been hard to understand, it was better that He went. If He did, the Lord would send the Holy Spirit to empower the disciples for their mission, and to convict the world concerning the message they were to share. In fact, Jesus said it's "better" that I go, and to expect very soon that the Spirit would come upon their lives.

I can imagine Jesus' leaving left them feeling at least a little uneasy, but to this point, they'd also learned they could trust Jesus. If He said it's better that He leaves, then I'm sure it's better. Based on Jesus' promise they expected the Holy Spirit's arrival, but they didn't just sit around and wait. With anticipation, they continually came together and prayed (Acts 1:14), and the Spirit came.

As they devoted themselves to preaching the message of Jesus, they ran into opposition. In fact, Peter and John were arrested, dragged before the court, severely threatened, and ordered to never even speak of Jesus. Following this encounter, Peter and John went directly to their friends, and whereas we may, in a similar situation, be intimidated or tempted to fear, Jesus' disciples were emboldened. They knew that God would take care of them and work through them, if they would rely on the power of the Spirit.

They didn't pray, "God, things have become dangerous—keep us safe," or, "Father, we need You to get us out of here." The spirit of their prayer was probably something like this: "God, give us the grace to proclaim the truth of Jesus so that Your mission will be fulfilled and others will come to know You." As these believers poured out their hearts in prayer, the place began to shake, the Spirit once again filled these disciples in a special way, and they were empowered to preach clearly and boldly.

Today, if we faithfully share the message of Jesus, we will face resistance. But, just like the first disciples, our mission is to proclaim the gospel. We're inadequate to make any difference on our own, but by the power of the Spirit, we can be used by God to change lives, and this depends in a big way on our living in prayerful dependence upon Him. Pray! Share! And when things are hard. Pray more.

When you think of sharing your faith, what about it seems scary?

What sorts of resistance have you faced when sharing your faith? How did you respond?

What role do you see prayer playing in helping you to remain steadfast in sharing the gospel when you face resistance?

PRAY WITH JESUS

Father, I know that the world naturally rages against You and Your message. Help me to live by the Spirit, that when I face resistance, I may be bold in living for You and lovingly sharing Your truth with others.

JOURNAL YOUR OWN PRAYER:

"Pray at all times in the Spirit with every prayer and request, and stay alert with all perseverance and intercession for all the saints." **EPHESIANS 6:18**

Somewhere and sometime, people got together and decided that students in the U.S. should go to school 180 days per year for twelve years. That's a lot of time devoted to learning. If given the choice, how many of those days would you have stayed home, and how many of those days would you have dragged yourself out of bed and toward another day of book-bagging and pencil-pushing? Some students love school, but many don't. If we invested in learning only when we felt like it, we'd miss out on the positive effect that comes from working diligently day-in, day-out. There's no arguing with the value associated with a great education, and the time spent on our educations opens many opportunities for a fulfilling future.

In Ephesians 6, Paul shared that the Christian life is, in many ways, like fighting a war. We may not have literal bombs and bullets flying at us, but we can be sure that there are, in the spiritual realm, weapons being continually used against God's people. In order to live victoriously, we have to arm ourselves according to the equipment God supplies. Paul shares an amazing list of pieces of armor at our disposal we are to use in attacking and defending against the forces of darkness— the belt of truth, helmet of salvation, and sword of the Spirit, to name a few. But Paul doesn't move on without mentioning, "Pray at all times."

The armor God provides is essential in keeping us safe in a world that is fiercely opposed to God, but Scripture is very clear that even these aren't enough to defend against the attacks of the enemy. In order to live successfully through the temptations we face, we must depend on the power of the Spirit. Prayer is in a sense, our saying, "God, I can't handle this on my own. I need you to be my strength, my Defender." Whenever we need to live by the power of God, we should pray—Paul says this is "at all times."

Further, we're to pray "with every prayer." In school, you study English, History, Art, Math, and many more subjects. Further, you don't just study Math in general, but many kinds of math— Algebra, Geometry, Calculus, and so on. If you want to be well-rounded and well-prepared for any number of opportunities and challenges life presents, it's important to have a broad range of skills and experience. We should, similarly, pray in ways that will help us be in the best position to succeed. We should pray alone and with our friends, with our families and small groups, and in church gatherings. We should pray over meals, in the car, when we wake up, before school, before bed, and every other occasion. As we pray, we should continually aware of the ways the devil would tempt us and draw us away from God. It's possible to pray in the flesh—prayers characterized by asking for things that would make us successful or comfortable in an earthly sense. In Luke 22:42 when Jesus prayed, "Not my will, but yours, be done," He denied His own immediate desires, surrendering instead to the Father as the Spirit led Him. Praying in the Spirit involves pursuing God's will, and being ever-ready to lay aside our own ideas and desires.

The ultimate goal of the Christ-follower is that God would rule in our lives, and that He'd use us to influence others toward this same end. Victory depends not only upon our learning to use the armor that God supplies, but also on living continually in prayer. If Jesus needed to pray in order to resist the devil and live in obedience to the Father, how much more do we need to pray?

In what ways have you experienced spiritual attacks?

In what ways do you use the armor of God when you face temptations and difficulties?

In your own words, how do you think prayer specifically helps us experience victory?

PRAY WITH JESUS

Father, I understand that I live in a world that's opposed to You, and is against me inasmuch as I seek to follow You. I'm too weak to succeed on my own, and I need You to protect me, and to provide the strength I need to live for You.

JOURNAL YOUR OWN PRAYER:

DEVO // DAY 5

"If you then, who are evil, know how to give good gifts to your children, how much more will the heavenly Father give the Holy Spirit to those who ask him?" **LUKE 11:13**

Parents, in many ways, like to spoil their children. How many moms and dads have driven halfway across the country and spent thousands of dollars to that their kids can hug a princess and get a hat with mouse ears? How many parents stress about the bills, all the while, they can't help but spend hundreds of dollars (or more) on Christmas presents for their little ones? Why do parents do this? Because they love their kids, and they want us to experience the good things life has to offer. In what ways have your parents spoiled you?

In case you didn't know (and I hate to break it to you), our parents aren't perfect. In fact, Jesus says that all earthly parents are "evil." Wow—that's tough. What Jesus means may not be necessarily be what immediately comes to mind. When we think of evil, we think of someone who's nasty and hateful, and who does terrible things to other people. But Jesus is saying that, for even the most loving people, when compared with God, they pale in comparison and their kindness is much closer to evil than God's infinite goodness.

Earthly parents are responsible to love, and teach, and care for their children, and most take this job seriously. So when their child asks for something they need, the parent does all he can to provide for that need. These "good gifts" are to characterize the relationship between a parent and child. But Jesus says that our heavenly Father, whose resources are unlimited and whose love is beyond measure, can provide for our needs so much better than even the best parents.

However, we often go without, which actually seems pretty silly. When we ask God for the things we need, especially when the things we ask for are in line with the Spirit's leading us, God is happy to provide it—every time! There's nothing that pleases God more than to hear His children asking for the things they need to mature spiritually and to grow closer to Him, and then to answer those prayers. However, we're often content to limp along, struggling with the same old sins that have haunted us for years, because we fail to ask for God's help. We miss out on so many good things God has for us because we just don't ask (James 4:2).

Jesus knew of God's plan to redeem humanity, and of the weight of what lay before Him. He also knew He'd need the Spirit's help to successfully fulfill what the Father required, so He prayed. He asked God to make the nations His inheritance, and to give the Holy Spirit, and His heavenly Father answered.

What "big ask" have you recently made of your parents? How did they respond?

What good gifts (not necessarily "things" or possessions) have your parents given you? How do these let you know your parents love you?

What good things has God given you as a result of your asking?

How do you need to change your prayer life, asking God for good spiritual things, knowing that He's happy to provide?

PRAY WITH JESUS

Father, I understand that I don't have certain good things in my life because I simply don't ask. Please help me to understand the specific things I need in order to grow, and provide those that I would live for You. Thank You for generously providing all I need.

JOURNAL YOUR OWN PRAYER:

Session 2
IN DESERTED PLACES

Focal Passage // Luke 5:15-16

Memory Verse // 1 Thessalonians 5:17
Pray constantly.

Weekly Reading // Luke 4:14–5:16

Like most people, I'm a music lover. When I was a young teenager, I had a number of chores around our home, and if I covered my responsibilities (and I usually did), I'd get just enough allowance to by a new CD—which I bought every week! Fast forward a few years, and I studied music in college. After graduating, in one way or another I played music for a living for the better part of two decades. Today, one of the great joys in my life is hearing great bands play live, and recently, I had the opportunity to see my favorite band of all time live at Nationals Park in Washington, D.C., with 40,000 of my closest friends. It was an incredible time! However, when I got home, I was worn out. Maybe it's because I sang along with every word for over three hours. Or maybe it's due to the fact that I'm extremely introverted, and being in a crowd wears me out.

How do you typically behave when you're in a crowd?

The most famous bands in the world have a way of drawing a crowd, and you've no doubt seen images of the paparazzi hounding celebrities as they look to go about their lives. However, even in today's technologically driven world, this doesn't begin to compare with the sort of following Jesus experienced. When Jesus showed up, He didn't play a mean guitar solo or deliver a line with dramatic flair. He miraculously turned water to wine and multiplied a boy's lunch to feed thousands. He healed people with chronic illnesses and freed those who were possessed by demons. He raised the dead!

Imagine the ever-increasing buzz surrounding Jesus as He went about His daily life. He loved people—after all, that's why He came. However, He would not (and could not) do so without continuing in relationship with the Father and Holy Spirit. The crowds were there to get, get, get—and Jesus gave—but through His connection within the Trinity, Jesus received relationally and spiritually the strength and encouragement to carry on.

At the concert, I wasn't even the center of attention, and it still took a toll. When Jesus walked the earth, He was not only the center of the crowds' attention—He was the center of attention of all the universe. Pouring Himself out in this way certainly had its costs, but Jesus was happy to do it. The way He dealt with these pressures, the way He remained energized, was to steal away and to stay prayerfully engaged with His heavenly Father.

WATCH

Watch this session's video, and then continue to the group discussion section using the content provided.

THE EXPANDING CROWDS

Some folks are *life-of-the-party* types. These are the joke-makers, leg-shakers, or risk-takers who make life exciting. Others are wallflowers who would rather go back to a flip-phone (oh, the horror!) than be the center of attention. Some are popular, admired, and celebrated. Others are unknown, ignored, or outcast.

In relation to these ideas, how would you describe yourself most of the time?

Scripture describes Jesus as a man of suffering who was well acquainted with sickness and grief; He was someone people turned away from; He was despised and rejected (Isa. 53:3). This doesn't sound like someone who was very popular, does it? When it was all said and done, these things were absolutely true—very few people bought in to counting the cost and taking up their cross for the sake of following Jesus. However, in Luke 5, we read the crowds were pursuing Jesus, and His popularity was increasing throughout the region.

From the time He was a young boy, people couldn't help but notice His ability to understand and communicate the Scriptures (Luke 2:46-47). When Jesus returned from being tempted in the wilderness, He began doing ministry in Galilee. All He pursued was by the power of the Spirit, including teaching in the synagogues, the places Jews gathered for teaching and worship. Those who heard Him were struck by the authority with which He taught, and people began proverbially singing His praises as they spoke of Jesus to others.

As Jesus traveled from town to town, He ran into people who were suffering beneath the weight of sin. For those who were spiritually oppressed, He rebuked the evil spirits and set people free. For the many who were sick, He healed them. We see throughout Scripture that is was not uncommon for Jesus to instruct those He healed to keep quiet about it. This may seem strange—after all, wasn't Jesus' purpose for us to tell about Him? Today, that's the case, but not at this point in the narrative.

In one particular instance, Jesus healed a man with leprosy, and as He did at other times, Jesus told the man, "See that you say nothing to anyone" (Mark 1:44). Jesus didn't want more and more people coming to Him at that time. He wanted to avoid the crowds and attention. However, the man didn't follow Jesus' instruction, and he went out telling everyone he saw about what Jesus had done for him. The result—word spread like wildfire, and from that point forward, Jesus couldn't go anywhere without being swarmed by multitudes.

The people wanted Jesus—at least they wanted the benefits He had to offer—and there was a non-stop stream of those asking for it. Today, life places many demands on us, and we certainly feel overwhelmed or stretched thin at times. Jesus always dealt graciously and effectively with these challenges because He made it a point to prioritize the most important things.

How does life press in on you and keep you from living in prayerful connection with God?

DESERTED PLACES

Many people live for the occasional moments life has to offer. We look forward to trips to the beach or our favorite band's next concert, getting a new puppy or our birthdays. Maybe we simply look forward to Friday! What's something you're really looking forward to?

We often see everything in between as the boring ho-hum existence we have to trudge through in order to make it to the next big thing. But if this is the way we see life, we miss out on so much of what God has for us. Excitement can be good, but let's be honest—life isn't about chasing the thrill, and when we do this, we become calloused and ungrateful in regard to the gifts God sends our way every day.

Jesus certainly experienced highlights—after all, I'm sure the energy among the crowds as Jesus served and healed was electric. In our passage, Jesus had just cleansed a leper and soon, He would heal a paralyzed man. Imagine what an experience that would be. When we experience successes, we're often tempted to revel in the limelight. Jesus, however, concerned Himself not with the attention of the crowds, but with the relationship with His Father. He didn't get caught up in all the excitement, but instead looked forward to stepping away from all of the clamor, and being in the stillness available only in deserted places. And it wasn't only because He was worn out and wanted a nap. What drove Him into isolation was His deep desire to engage personally and prayerfully with His Father.

Scripture calls us to pray constantly (1 Thess. 5:17). The idea here, as gross as it may sound, is that of a hacking cough. When we're sick, coughing is something that just happens. Sure, we can control it to an extent, but it's always bubbling just beneath the surface ready to burst through. Prayer should be like this—something that continually and habitually happens as a natural expression of our being connected with God.

We'll all experience our big moments, but most of life consists of the ordinary everyday, and how we fill those moments goes a long way in determining our spiritual wellness. We're often quick to fight off boredom with watching internet videos or scrolling through our social media feeds, but Jesus "often" withdrew in order to feed His soul on the faithful and unwavering goodness of His Father. He "constantly" prayed because there was nothing else He'd rather do.

What is something you constantly do that gives insight into where your heart finds satisfaction? What does this say about your connection with God?

ALONE WITH THE FATHER

When we're born, we're totally dependent upon our parents. We can't communicate very well—we cry when we're hungry, and scream when we're mad, and wave our limbs about (who knows what that means?). We can't feed ourselves. We can't get around at all—we can't even roll over. We depend on mom and dad for everything. As we grow, we depend less and less on our parents, to the point we're in middle school and we know everything—and mom and dad know nothing—right? What three words best describe your relationship with your parents?

Since creation, people are designed to live in relationship with one another. We're shaped to have family and friends, to be intimately connected with a spouse, and to be close with fathers and mothers, sons and daughters. Personally, I have an incredibly strong connection with my dad. It started from my earliest memories. When I was three years old, I can remember my dad pitching a whiffle ball to me in our front yard, and if I hit it over our neighbor's 1979 Trans Am, it was considered over the wall (I hit the car a few times, but our neighbor didn't care!). I started playing Tee-ball when I was five, and every time I hit a home run in real life, our team's players and parents would go crazy, but as I rounded the bases, seeing my dad's expression of pride meant more to me than everyone else put together.

But the moments that mean the most to me aren't my dad's yelling in celebration of my success on the baseball diamond. It's the summer afternoons my dad spent pitching to me after a long day at work. It's the time on the lake when I was a teenager. It's his helping me with homework, or grilling burgers for my friends, or taking us to the movies.

Relationships are built on time and communication—the small everyday moments. Jesus had lived for eternity past in intimate relationship with His Father in heaven, and when He came to earth, He wasn't about to let that change. As much as earthly parents and children love each other, this doesn't compare to the affection and devotion Jesus has for His Father. Jesus truly loved the people in the crowds, but they came to Him to take, and it was physically and emotionally draining. However, during His time with the Father, Jesus was fed and filled and energized to continue on with the demanding ministry for which He came.

When Jesus was born, He was dependent upon His earthly father and mother, just like the rest of us. As He grew into adulthood, He grew into personal independence as. However, Jesus is unique among people in the ways He remained connected with and dependent upon the Father. We're generally happy, because of human pride, to depend on ourselves, both in an earthly and in a spiritual sense. However, the truth is we can do nothing for ourselves. All we have comes from God, including our abilities and opportunities. Jesus knew this, and remained continually connected with the Father—He prayed constantly because He loved Him, and He needed these moments to be filled and encouraged.

Considering relationships are built on time and communication, how strong do you think your relationship is with God?

1. The Expanding Crowds

Students today face more pressure than at any time in history. Schedules can get out of control, with the advanced classes and hours of homework, long sports practices, and chores at home. And on top of this, you feel the obligation to be a church, spend time in accountability and encouragement, and study your Bible and pray. Wow!

What pressures are causing you to feel overwhelmed right now?

What can you learn from Jesus about how to respond in times like this?

2. Deserted Places

Jesus' ministry was naturally associated with pressures that are simply unimaginable to us, and because Jesus was a real man, He felt it in real ways. Whereas we often deal with pressure in unhealthy ways, Jesus models for us the perfect way to deal with life's pressures.

When you feel like you need a break from it all, where do you find comfort?

What value is there in sharing our hearts with God when we feel overwhelmed?

3. Alone with the Father

We're created as social beings. We enjoy going to ball games, celebrating victories with the thousands, and we enjoy long private conversations one-on-one. This is expressed in our faith life as well. We worship corporately and privately, and both are essential to our spiritual growth. Jesus demonstrated that, central to everything else is the intimate personal relationship with the Father.

How have you learned the value of the continual, everyday interactions with those you love?

How would God have you grow in cultivating the continual, personal connection with Him?

PRAY LIKE JESUS

Take a few minutes now and pray:

- That God would give you a growing influence among your friends and neighbors
- That the Father would give you times of solitude, stillness, and rest from the busyness of life
- That you would continually grow in intimacy with God

"... and my people, who bear my name, humble themselves, pray and seek my face, and turn from their evil ways, then I will hear from heaven, forgive their sin, and heal their land. My eyes will now be open and my ears attentive to prayer from this place." **2 CHRONICLES 7:14-15**

I have kids and they have a bedtime. There are certain occasions when my wife and I are really lenient in enforcing it, such as all summer long! However, there are also times (such as when Dad has to get up really early) we communicate very clearly that it's important the kids go to bed and be quiet. Recently, despite their repeatedly asking, our three girls for some reason or other thought it was best that, for another two hours, they continue to talk, giggle, and dance! So they were rewarded with the privilege of getting up at 5:30 a.m. for the foreseeable future.

God's people, though He had been extremely good to them, had time and time again disobeyed God. And this wasn't just a minor slip up—their disobedience was a sign of lack of faith in God. Their choices were a clear reflection of their hearts, and it wasn't a picture of love and devotion to their good Father.

God had promised them that, if they lived in continual obedience, He would bless them (Deut. 11:26-28). And they had seen Him deliver. When they'd groaned beneath Egyptian oppression, God miraculously freed them. When they wandered in the desert, He led them. When then were hungry and thirsty, He fed them and provided them with water. He'd given them military victory, and an amazing land to call their own. And perhaps most importantly, He'd given them the law that they would not only know how to live, but they'd also know the character of the God they served.

However, God warned that if they turned away, in place of the blessing, they'd receive a curse. It seems pretty simple, right? God is super-good, and when we live in obedience, He continually blesses us, so let's do what He says. But that's not the way it worked out. God's people were tempted by things that were outside God's plan for them, and their hearts were turned. After being incredibly patient, because of His justice, God was forced into disciplining His people.

It's important that we pay attention to this idea. Discipline is different than punishment. Punishment is retribution (or payback) for the sake of inflicting suffering for past wrongs. Because of their choices, God had the right to inflict severe punishment. But instead, He chose discipline—consequences intended to modify behavior. Make no mistake, there were consequences for Israel's disobedience. However, all along, God was inviting them to return to Him, and He told Solomon, the king who built the temple where worship would be established, *"I have heard your prayer and have chosen this place for myself as a temple of sacrifice. If I shut the sky so there is no rain, or if I command the grasshopper to consume the land, or if I send pestilence on my people, and my people, who bear my name, humble themselves, pray and seek my face, and turn from their evil ways, then I will hear from heaven, forgive their sin, and heal their land"* (2 Chr. 7:12b-14).

Here's what God was saying. Because my people have sinned, I've had to discipline you. But because you've prayed with a right heart, if the nation is willing to be humble and turn away from their sins, I'm ready to forgive and restore.

Though my girls can get a little crazy, particularly at bedtime, the truth is that I find no pleasure in seeing them suffer by getting up really early (okay, maybe just a little). But the truth is, when they learn to follow my instruction—which is legitimately for their own benefit (when they stay up late, getting up for school is hard, and they drag all day, and complain that school is tough, and on and on)—I'm happy to let them return to their normal sleep schedule. In fact, I want this for them, because it's best for everyone.

Living in relationship with God involves continually choosing to turn away from the world and from sin, and pursuing God Himself as the ultimate blessing.

What tempts you to turn away from God and His will for your life?

How have you experienced God's discipline in the past?

For you personally, how would God have you:

- **Humble yourself?**

- **Pray?**

- **Seek His face?**

- **Turn away from sin?**

PRAY WITH JESUS

Father, thank You for being patient with me when I sin, and when I turn away to the point that I need correction, thank You for being willing to restore me when I repent. Help me to desire You above all other things.

JOURNAL YOUR OWN PRAYER:

"The LORD will send his faithful love by day; his song will be with me in the night—a prayer to the God of my life." **PSALM 42:8**

One of my favorite pastimes is hiking, and every year I do my best to make it to Colorado to hike a couple 14ers—mountains over 14,000 feet. I still wonder sometimes why I do this, because, whereas at 6 a.m. when I hit the trail I feel great, after six hours and six miles of walking continually uphill—and when the air has about half the oxygen of what I'm used to in Baltimore—I feel less than terrific. In all honesty, here's what's really going on—I still have to walk back down the mountain on legs that are completely burned out, and moved by a will that's been all but shattered by the ascent. As I literally gasp for oxygen, there's nothing more I want than to be in my recliner in front of the TV, and at sea level where I can breathe.

In Psalm 42, we get a peek into the mind of a man who knows God, and who has undoubtedly experienced good times, but who is currently facing indescribably difficult struggles. In the first eight verses, David describes his situation like this:

- The only food I've had to eat is my tears (v. 3).

- People are continually mocking me, asking, "Where is this God you say you believe in?" (v. 3)

- My soul is discouraged and hopeless (v. 5).

- I'm full of worry and anxiety (v. 5).

- I'm depressed (v. 6).

- And I feel like God's the one drowning me with all these troubles (v. 7).

Sounds like a pretty tough spot, right? David remembers a time when he had experienced the joy of gathering with friends and family, worshiping God, and celebrating the many good things God had poured out on his life. However, those things seem far removed from his current condition, and he's gasping for the grace and goodness of God as if he's drowning beneath violently crashing waves. Nonetheless, David knows that the Lord possesses an infinite supply of love and kindness, and He will send it to His children in due time.

As Jesus began His public ministry, He not only faced demands from the growing crowds and the violent hatred of Israel's religious leaders, but He for the first time in all of eternity felt the weakness associated with the human condition. Jesus surely remembered sweet moments over meals with His family, or worshiping with other faithful followers in the synagogue in which He thought, *isn't my Father good?* However, as His suffering intensified, and as those good times seemed to belong in the distant past, Jesus longed for the refreshing that came only from intimacy with God.

When we experience difficult times—and we will—there are an infinite number of ways we seek to comfort ourselves and fill our longings. Many of those are unhealthy and lead to deeper despair and suffering. However, we must recognize that God created us with an ultimate longing for Him, and when we experience longing, God is the one thing that will meaningfully fill it.

When the psalmist suffered, He longed for God, and as He pursued God in worship and prayer, He trusted that God would again bless Him. When Jesus felt the pressure of serving others' demands, He pursued the Father in worship and prayer, knowing this was the one thing that would fill Him. When we experience the challenges and pressures of this life, one non-negotiable we must pursue is prayer.

What "waves" have you experienced recently crashing on your life?

What, good or bad, do you naturally long for to provide comfort?

How is God calling you to grow in your longing for Him?

PRAY WITH JESUS

Father, this life is full of pressures and challenges, and the only way I can endure it successfully is to live in continual dependence on You. When I'm emotionally and spiritually hungry and thirsty, help me to turn to You to fill me. Thank You for supplying all my needs!

JOURNAL YOUR OWN PRAYER:

"They devoted themselves to the apostles' teaching, to the fellowship, to the breaking of bread, and to prayer." **ACTS 2:42**

If we want to be successful in most any pursuit, there are certain things that are required. For instance, to play piano at a high level requires, at the very least, learning the notes and keys, an understanding of music, and practicing every day. To be a stellar athlete requires working out to become strong, eating well to keep the body healthy, learning techniques, and practicing every day. Succeeding at geometry requires mastering math principles, learning to use a compass and protractor, and studying every day.

The early days of the church were incredibly important, not just for those who were a part of it then, but in an eternal perspective. And in order for the church to thrive, certain things had to happen:

- **Scripture:** The church devoted themselves to the teaching of the apostles, and what they taught were the doctrines of the Old Testament Scriptures, as well as the truth about Jesus. The people were hungry to know the truth and they were motivated to live by what they learned.

- **Fellowship:** These Christians had a lot in common—they had devoted their lives to Christ and shared the same eternal hope, the same desire to honor God and turn from sinful ways, and even the same people set against them. They were knit together by these shared experiences.

- **Communion:** Sharing meals is a sign of good relationships. Close families often enjoy family meals, friends often visit each other's homes or go out to eat together, and in the early church, because of the close fellowship they experienced, they regularly shared meals together. However, there was more to it—they also made it a point to remember the sacrifice of Christ. Just as Jesus had commanded (Luke 22:19-20), they continually received the bread and the cup as an act of worship and remembrance. Jesus was central to their fellowship.

One final component that was necessary to the church's thriving was prayer. Just as Jesus came into the world and experienced hardship and suffering, He knew the church was being sent out like sheep among wolves (Matt. 10:16). The benefits of being in it together were indescribable. However, in order to thrive, they were going to need supernatural strength and encouragement. This could come only from a deep connection with God, and prayer was central to this.

These weren't things they did just when they were starting out, because things were fresh and because they were excited. The church continued steadfastly in all these, because each was necessary for the kingdom to advance and for Christ's purposes to be accomplished in their lives, both individually and collectively. With this in view, they prayed in their closets alone. They prayed with their families in the morning and before bedtime. They prayed with their friends over meals and in their living rooms. They prayed publicly in church gatherings. They prayed for the lost and for the sick. They prayed for their leaders and for the government.

That they were devoted to prayer and other disciplines means they understood the inherent value, committed to these, and followed through. For us to experience success in the Christian life the way God intends, we need not only see the value in prayer and commit to it—we have to follow through continually. Jesus exemplified it. The early church practiced it. Now let's follow in their example.

What's something you've proven you're devoted to?

In your own words, describe what it would look like to be devoted to prayer?

Why was it so important that the early church continued steadfastly in prayer? How does the same apply to you?

PRAY WITH JESUS

Father, I understand that being a follower of Christ means that I'm continually devoted to You and Your will. Thank You for giving me the strength to live well in the middle of a crooked world. Help me to practice Christian disciplines so that I may continue to stand strong.

JOURNAL YOUR OWN PRAYER:

"This is the confidence we have before him: If we ask anything according to his will, he hears us. And if we know that he hears whatever we ask, we know that we have what we have asked of him." **1 JOHN 5:14-15**

Growing up, I loved green beans. In fact, the ones I picked out of my grandfather's garden and that my grandmother prepared were the absolute best! If my parents ever asked me what I wanted to eat, green beans were always on the list. If I'd said, peanut butter cups, or ice cream, they probably would have let me have it from time to time. After all, things like this are okay in moderation. However, every time I answered that what I really wanted was a green vegetable—which they had taught me to appreciate, which is super healthy, and which most parents have to force young kids to eat—their answer was a resounding yes!

Throughout history, God has revealed certain aspects of His will to people:

- **Creation:** He called Adam and Eve to multiply and spread God's image bearers throughout the earth. He also gave them instructions to rule over the earth in reflecting His authority.

- **The Law:** God gave commandments so that His people would know His character and how to live in order to have healthy, blessed lives and to display His character.

- **The Prophets:** God spoke through the prophets to remind His people about how they are to live and to warn them that, if they continued to disobey, they would be punished.

- **Individuals:** God spoke time and time again to individuals to reveal aspects of His will. He told Noah to build a ship, Abraham to travel to a foreign land, and Gideon to go to war with a small army. Scripture is filled with stories of God's specific calls on people's lives.

- **Jesus:** Most clearly, we see God and hear God's call through Jesus. All of God's Word ultimately points to Jesus.

The essence of following Christ is to live as He lived. Everything Jesus pursued was for the sake of fulfilling the Father's will (John 6:38), and to follow Christ means literally to walk in the will of God. The problem is, however, that what we want is not always what God wants. Jesus experienced this too. In His humanity, there were times that His flesh (not human "flesh," which is in bondage to sin, but the part of Jesus' nature that experienced temptation) tempted Him do depart from the path God had set before Him. Yet, every step along the way, He intentionally chose to do the Father's will.

Prayer is our way of intentionally conforming our desires to those of God. There will be times we're exhausted from life's busyness, and we'll be tempted to do things our own away instead of pressing forward according to God's plans. At times, others' expectations will weigh heavy, and we'll be tempted to do things to please them instead of pleasing God. Still, at other times, we'll simply desire the temporary pleasures offered by sin instead of the eternal pleasures God offers. Whatever the case, the way we can make sure we're staying on track is to, like Jesus did, is to devote ourselves continually to prayer.

We know God's revealed will by studying Scripture. But the Bible doesn't give specific instructions for every detail of our lives. As we gain knowledge by studying the Scripture, and as we pray that God would help us to know and live out His will, that knowledge is translated into wisdom—knowing how to walk in God's will according to principle and when it's not specified.

And here's the beauty of it all. When we ask God to give us those things, He's already revealed He desires for us, He's happy to say yes! In fact, when we ask for those, it's as if we already have them.

What are some things you know God desires in your life that you're not currently living by?

Not only ask for those things, but also let your life and actions demonstrate you want them. How will you show God this week that you desire to follow His will?

PRAY WITH JESUS

Father, I'm thankful that You are faithful, and that I can have confidence You'll provide what I need when I pursue Your will. Help me to know Your desires, not only in the big picture, but also for my life specifically, and help me to live like Jesus in following Your desires.

JOURNAL YOUR OWN PRAYER:

"Whenever you pray, you must not be like the hypocrites, because they love to pray standing in the synagogues and on the street corners to be seen by people. Truly I tell you, they have their reward. But when you pray, go into your private room, shut your door, and pray to your Father who is in secret. And your Father who sees in secret will reward you." **MATTHEW 6:5-6**

Some of us like to be the center of attention, and others are more timid, but whether we admit it or not, we all like to receive praise. In fact, we were created to receive glory—not the glory of men, but that of being known by God. However, because of sin, we've gotten this mixed up, and today many pursue prestige and fame above all other things.

In Jesus' day, those who had been given the responsibility of spiritual oversight among God's people had this specific problem. There were many people who looked to them for insights about how to know God, and how to live in order to be blessed by Him. But instead of acknowledging the weight of such a responsibility and directing the glory to God—to whom it was rightly due—they would flaunt their piety and seek to impress others with their vast spiritual knowledge and insightful prayers. The crowds would "Ooh" and "Ahh," and the Pharisees would puff their chests in pride. But tragically, the Lord was not pleased.

Today, it can be tempting to do the same thing. It may not look exactly the same. After all, we don't dress in ways to show off our religious devotion, we don't demand that others call us Rabbi or Holy Father when they address us, and we're not standing on street corners and praying out loud for others to hear. But we don't, from time to time, mind telling about how hard we worked on the summer mission trip, or sharing that we gave a few dollars to the homeless guy, or coming up with just the right words to say when we pray in our group, concerned more with what our friends think than truly sharing our heart with God.

Sometimes, I think we can take Jesus' call to pray (and fast, and give) in secret a little too far. We may be tempted to think that we can never even share about fasting or generously giving to meet others' needs. This simply isn't the case, and sometimes our obedience in these regards can inspire others to do the same. After all, praying out loud before others isn't a sin.

Ultimately, it's not about whether or not others know we do these things. In fact, for Christians, others should naturally assume we do all these and more. The question isn't if, by why? If we're fasting to make people think we're super spiritual, our motives are all wrong. If we're giving to impress others, we've missed the point. And if our prayers are for the sake of making ourselves look good, we are missing out on the benefit of connecting with God in a meaningful way.

Jesus prayed many times in the presence of others. When He did, it was never to impress, but to connect with or appeal to His Father in heaven. However, when the pressures of life and ministry became hard to bear, His most natural inclination was to get away to a private place and engage one on one with the God He loved so deeply. This is the heart of prayer—to engage honestly with God with no concern for what others think. When God meets children with a deep longing to engage in this way, He pours out unimaginable blessings on our lives.

How can we know when it's okay to pray before others and when it's not?

When have you been tempted to pursue spiritual things to impress others?

When you've done things for no earthly recognition, how have you experienced God rewarding you?

PRAY WITH JESUS

Father, I'm sometimes tempted to do right things for the wrong reasons. Please help me to be satisfied in You and not in the praise of other people.

JOURNAL YOUR OWN PRAYER:

Session 3
ALL NIGHT IN PRAYER

Focal Passage // Luke 6:12

Memory Verse // James 1:5

Now if any of you lacks wisdom, he should ask God—who gives to all generously and ungrudgingly—and it will be given to him.

Weekly Reading // Luke 5:17-6:49

Per the definition, .006 percent of the population (that's six out of 100,000 people) are geniuses.[1] This means a few of us are pretty smart, and the rest of us aren't nearly as smart as we think we are! Fortunately, God has surrounded us with people who have, in relation to ourselves, a lot more knowledge and life-experience, wisdom and plain ol' common sense. God designed us all to learn and grow, and one way or the other, we're going to learn lessons throughout our lifetime. There's the "hard way"—doing things our own way until, through trial and error, we figure out a thousand things that don't work in identifying the one that does. Then there's the much easier way—learning from the wisdom of others.

What's a lesson you've learned the hard way?

Every person on the planet needs others to help us grow in knowledge and skills. In my life, I've had a number of mentors who've influenced my decisions and helped shape my life. As a musician, I had a professor in college who helped me learn not only technique and good musicianship, but to have confidence in myself. As a pastor, I had a mentor who helped me grow in theological knowledge and communication skills, and perhaps more importantly, in relating well to people. I have a long list of teachers and coaches, pastors and mentors who've influenced me. And of course, my mom and dad have, over the years, poured more wisdom and insights into me than I can even begin to appreciate (and believe me, I recognize that they've given me a lot!).

Even to this day, I quite frequently call my mom and dad with questions about all sorts of issues. This is because, despite that I'm a grown man and responsible to take care of myself and my family, they have a wealth of wisdom and life experience, and I can lean into them to help me make good choices.

Despite that Jesus is God in the flesh, during His time on earth, He set aside certain powers and privileges in order to experience humanity in its fullness. This required His living in dependence upon the Father for wisdom to make good decisions. Day in and day out, Jesus made choices that would impact the world in significant ways. Some decisions were especially important, and Jesus felt the weight of these. He could have carried these burdens Himself, yet we see that He continually went to the Father for wisdom.

For the large majority of us, we're not part of the .006 percent of the population who are really smart. And even if we are, we're not even nearly as smart as Jesus. He leaned on God for wisdom, and we should too!

Watch this session's video, and then continue to the group discussion section using the content provided.

TO THE MOUNTAIN

The life of today's American teenager can be pretty hectic (for adults too). When the hustle and bustle begins to get to me, I like to vacate to the mountains for a nice hike. When I'm on my way up, I ask myself time and time again, "Why in the world do I do this?" Only a few miles in, my legs are jelly and I'm gasping for air (at 14,000 feet, there's significantly less oxygen as compared to sea level). But when I summit the mountain, the view—and the sense of accomplishment—make it worth every weary step and every labored breath.

What do you like to do when life gets tough?

Our focus verse says that "during those days," Jesus went to the mountain to pray. Let's talk about those days. We last saw Jesus praying in Luke 5:16. In the verses to follow, and leading up to where we are now, Jesus:

- Healed a paralytic (and forgave his sins!)
- Ate with Levi and a group of tax collectors (who were hated by the Jews)
- Picked some grain and ate a bite with His disciples
- Taught in a Jewish synagogue
- Healed a man with a shriveled hand—on the Sabbath!

Here's how the Pharisees responded. They accused Jesus of blasphemy—who can forgive sins but God alone? They complained that He associated with sinners—God's people are supposed to be set apart, not associating with pagans. They accused Him of breaking the law—He picked grain, and God's law says we can't work on the Sabbath. They were enraged that Jesus would compassionately heal a crippled man on the Sabbath—healing on the Sabbath—more work! In fact, the Pharisees were so furious at Jesus that they "started discussing with one another what they might do to Jesus" (Luke 6:11), and this didn't involve giving Him a day of rest and relaxation at the spa.

As Jesus lived out more and more fully the purposes He came to fulfill, because these didn't align with the desires of Israel's religious leaders, they grew to hate Him with an ever-growing intensity. After all, this young Teacher was messing up the system which for generations had allowed them to have things exactly as they wanted—and they weren't about to put up with Him!

As Jesus faced these pressures, He knew it was building toward the cross. After all, even at this point the religious leaders were intent on seeing Him destroyed—murdered! As the heat was turned up, Jesus needed support and encouragement, and He found these in His relationship with the Father. The disciples loved Jesus, but they just didn't get it. The crowds were continually clamoring for His attention and for His miracles. And Israel's leaders hated Him with all that was in them. Jesus' time in prayer was the fuel that helped Jesus push forward toward God's purposes through all the resistance, and the mountain provided the perfect place for Him to get away and engage one on one with His Father.

ALL NIGHT IN PRAYER

You wouldn't necessarily know it by looking at me today, but once upon a time I was in pretty good shape. Though it wasn't my favorite sport, I ran on my school's track team, primarily to stay in shape for other sports I played. Here's the problem. I wasn't quick enough to run sprints, and I wasn't in good enough shape to run distance races, so I was designated to run the 400 and 800 meter races—which many would argue are the most painful to run! Here's why. Sprinters push one hundred percent, but it's a short burst, and the race is over before it hurts too much. Distance runners go at a relaxed pace for much of the race and turn up the heat incrementally as the race nears the end. But middle distances require that runners go nearly all out, and when the lungs are on fire, the legs are screaming, and the body wants to give out, you've gotta push some more.

Hebrews 12:1 teaches the Christian life is like an endurance race. It's long and has its share of ups and downs. There are times when, spiritually speaking, we're feeling great, and others when we're struggling. But all in all, the intensity isn't always at a ten.

Jesus' earthly ministry was different. He came out of the gates going strong, and only pressed the throttle more as He went forward. His time with the disciples was intense. His preaching ministry was tenacious. His healing ministry, physically and spiritually speaking, was pursued with great urgency. He wasn't necessarily in a hurry as we often are—after all, He walked most places, but Jesus was certainly continually about His business, and He pursued God's purposes with an urgency and an intensity we'll never experience.

He prayed this way too. For us to think about praying all night may be an overwhelming thought. How many times have we set about to pray bedtime prayers, and fell asleep before we put together a cohesive thought? In a sense that's okay—what better way to go to sleep than while praying. However, to Jesus, prayer was far more important than sleep. His days were filled with ministry that were no doubt draining in every sense. And when it would have been most natural to sleep, He prayed. As opposition grew in intensity, and as the pace of life and ministry became more demanding, Jesus spent more and more time, not sleeping (or watching TV), but in prayer.

We may at times have the thought, *I'm just too busy to spend much time in prayer.* But if Jesus' life is any indication, when our schedules are at their busiest and life's demands are greatest, this isn't the time to relax, but to increase our devotion to prayer and communion with God.

IMPORTANT DECISIONS

Every year toward the end of school students are piled with reports and finals, papers and exams, presentations, and on and on. To top it off, as high school days come to a close, students are tasked with making life-altering decisions, like where to go to college, whether you should just get a job, or if it's time to marry the person you've dated the past two years. What's the biggest decision you've ever faced?

Not only was Jesus faced with the external pressures applied by the crowds and the religious leaders, He faced tremendous internal pressures as well. As He served the multitudes, Jesus preached the gospel and called people to leave behind lives devoted to their own purposes for the sake of following Him. And some did. For a select few of these disciples, God had a very special purpose—He'd use them to lay the foundation for the church Jesus would build for generations, even up to our time today.

Immediately following His time on the mountain, from those who had committed their lives to following Him, Jesus would select twelve apostles. For us, a decision regarding school, a job, or a relationship can be really difficult. And, don't get me wrong—these decisions are critically important. But this was one of the most critical moments of Jesus' life, and the fate of the world (literally) rested upon the choices Jesus made as He selected the apostles. And He relied on the wisdom of the Father in making these decisions.

If Jesus needed heavenly wisdom, how much more do we? For most of the decisions we make, we think very little of praying for God's perspectives. If we want a pack of gum, we buy it. If we want to see a new movie, we just go. If we want to ask a girl out, why not? Or if a boy asks us out [he's cute (blush)], of course! Which college? The one with my favorite campus. We tend to think that small decisions are insignificant. Concerning big ones, as long as we do our research, let our friends weigh in, and maybe even ask mom and dad, we simply do what we think is best. But the truth of the matter is, for small decisions, we should pray. For big decisions, pray more! In all decisions, as we pray without ceasing and express our reliance upon God, we'll be equipped with godly wisdom and we'll be prepared to navigate any challenges the world throws our way.

Jesus faced pressures from every side, and we see over and over that He relied on prayer to successfully live out the purposes of God in His life. Jesus provides the perfect example for the ways we're to face our own challenges. When the pressure was on, He prayed. He even made sacrifices to make it happen. Find your mountain. Pray!

How can you demonstrate dependence on God for the choices you make, both small and large?

1. To the Mountain

As Jesus served others according to the spirit of the law, He faced an ever-increasing resistance from the religious leaders. The pressures He felt were real, and the way He dealt with it was to get away to spend time with His Father. Regularly, these were relatively short moments, but at others Jesus needed an extended retreat.

When have you felt like you were doing the right thing, but others didn't understand?

How do you respond in these situations? How can you live in greater dependence on God?

2. All Night in Prayer

When we're extremely busy and we engage in activities that are heavily demanding—a big paper, football camp, or a long day skiing at the lake—we often refuel by sleeping in, vegging out on the couch all day, or by eating way too many cheese curls. Jesus, however, did it differently. He was emotionally and spiritually replenished by time with the Father.

Where do you usually turn when you're tired or down?

How is God calling you to grow in valuing prayer and a relationship with Him above worldly desires—even things like sleep or food?

3. Important Decisions

Every decision we make is important on some level. For smaller, everyday decisions, it's not necessarily important that we spend hours agonizing over which one is right. However, we are called to apply godly wisdom in all circumstances—*Is this shirt truly modest?*—and prayer helps us to be in tune with God, and helps us make good choices, big and small.

What are ways we're called to pursue wisdom from God?

How does your prayer life demonstrate that you truly desire to live according to God's wisdom? How will you commit to growing in this?

PRAY LIKE JESUS

Take a few minutes now and pray:
- That God would give you the desire and the discipline to regularly engage in prayer
- That God would help you to know when you need to pull back from all that keeps you busy in order to engage with Him

"I will bring them to my holy mountain and let them rejoice in my house of prayer. Their burnt offerings and sacrifices will be acceptable on my altar, for my house will be called a house of prayer for all nations." **ISAIAH 56:7**

The temple where God dwelled among His people was built upon the mountain in Jerusalem, and it had several specific areas:

- **Holy of Holies:** This was where the presence of God dwelled, and was separated from the rest of the temple by a veil. Only the high priest was allowed to enter (anyone else would die immediately), and even then, only once per year to offer a sacrifice for the sins of God's people.

- **Holy Place:** Contained the golden lampstand, the altar of incense, and the table of showbread that priests used in carrying out worship rituals. Because this area was close to God, all the elements were made of gold, and common worshipers were forbidden to enter.

- **Inner Court:** Here, all the elements, such as the altar where sacrifices were burned, were made of bronze. All Jewish people were allowed to enter, where they waited in reverence to offer their sacrifice to God.

- **Outer Court:** Whereas Jewish men could enter the Inner Court anytime, women could only enter when they came to offer a sacrifice. The Outer Court was the area of the temple where women would regularly gather for worship.

- **Court of Gentiles:** Gentiles (non-Jews) weren't allowed in the temple except in the outermost courtyard. The sick and poor who sought help would gather here, hoping to find compassion from God's people, and Gentiles who wanted to honor Israel's God would come here for worship.

As you can see, worship under the old covenant was much different than what we experience today. Connecting with God had far more restrictions than what we experience today. Only the priests could enter directly into God's presence, and even then only once a year. The common people could only approach God through the priests, and for Gentiles, as well as the sick and poor, they were left on the fringes.

This was bad news for people who wanted to be close to God, but who didn't meet the right qualifications. However, despite so many being cut off, God made a promise that gives hope to all people in Isaiah 56:7. The temple, which sat atop God's holy mountain, would be opened to all people! No matter our background or heritage, our struggles or ailments, if we're willing to find rest in Christ and honor God's covenant, we're invited into His presence.

This is something we may take for granted today, but we need never to lose sight of what a tremendous privilege this is. That His temple would be known as a house of prayer for all nations, not just for the Jews, would have been mind-blowing for many under the old covenant. Prayer implied a deep and personal connection with God.

Whereas before, many were excluded, God looked forward to a time when, because of Jesus' high priestly ministry, all people would have the privilege of entering the most holy place and directly into the presence of God. His temple—His people—is to be characterized by prayer, and when we approach Him in humility and reverence, we are accepted into His presence.

Jesus longed continually to be in the presence of His Father, and we find again and again, when the pressures of life began to weigh down on Him, Jesus would ascend the mountain into the presence of God to enjoy the intimate fellowship available to those committed to living for the Father's will.

When have you felt cut off from God?

According to God's promises, how can we know that we are welcome into God's presence?

How should we view our prayer life in light of this?

PRAY WITH JESUS

Father, because sin cannot be in Your presence, I understand that I have no right to come to You. However, because You've given me Jesus' righteousness, I'm accepted. Thank You! Help me to approach You in humility in reverence in light of this great privilege You've given to me.

JOURNAL YOUR OWN PRAYER:

"LORD, how my foes increase! There are many who attack me. Many say about me, 'There is no help for him in God.' But you, LORD, are a shield around me, my glory, and the one who lifts up my head. I cry aloud to the LORD, and he answers me from his holy mountain."
PSALM 3:1-4

When we live for God, we will experience trouble. Jesus warned this would be the case, and we can certainly see it today. For instance, in North Korea, if Christians are discovered, they are either deported to labor camps, or killed on the spot. In Afghanistan, those who convert to Christianity are labeled "insane" for leaving the Muslim faith. If they're families can't convince them to return to their former faith, they're either committed to a psychiatric institution, or beaten or killed by their own families. In our world today, every year:

- 3000 Christians are murdered,

- 1250 are abducted,

- 2150 Christian women are raped or forced into marriage,

- 800 churches are attacked,

- and 2000 Christians are imprisoned without a trial[2]

We may not experience trouble the same way people do in other parts of the world. However, U.S. Christians' values certainly don't align with those of the mainstream, and more and more, we're seeing the culture coming against the church and its values.

When David ruled Israel, He did some things really well, and God blessed Him! He also made some huge mistakes, which got him into some messy situations. He had many children by multiple wives (1 Chr. 3:1-8), and because David didn't love and lead them as a father should, as we would expect, they didn't all get along.

On one occasion, one of David's sons, Absalom, conspired against his father to take over the kingdom, and as the conspiracy grew, David was the one with reason to fear for his life. David wrote Psalm 3 while he was running from Absalom, his son who was intent on murdering him, and he spoke of trouble out of real experience.

When we experience hardship, it may be difficult to see how or when things may ever get better. In America today, things are a lot different than they were even a few years ago. Our culture is one that is becoming increasingly hostile toward Christian values, and if we state our perspectives concerning things like marriage, gender, abortion, or other sensitive issues, we are sure to be met with accusations of being hateful or intolerant. And it may appear as if there is no way things will ever turn around. In fact, it may seem as if things are getting worse all the time.

David likely felt like this in a certain sense. After all, one of his own children was out for his life! Nonetheless, he held on to God's promises, and he recognized that, because God is in control and will accomplish His purposes, things would certainly get better in God's time.

For those who are part of God's family, He is our shield. When we're overwhelmed with trouble, He rescues and lifts us up with love and encouragement. And when we cry to Him from the depths of the valley, weighed down by our sin, even though He is high and exalted upon His holy mountain, He bends down to hear us. When life is difficult, our first instinct should be to do exactly what David did—cry out to God. He hears us, and because He cares, He will answer.

In what ways have you experienced others coming against you because of your faith?

Describe a time when you felt like things were so bad it could never get better.

When we pray, God answers from His holy mountain. How should this idea affect the way you pray?

PRAY WITH JESUS

Father, the mountain where you dwell is a holy place where I don't belong. However, You allow me to come to You because You love me, and because Jesus paid the price for my sin. Help me to trust that, because of Your goodness toward Your people, You'll take care of me.

JOURNAL YOUR OWN PRAYER:

DEVO // DAY 3

"Then they prayed, 'You, Lord, know everyone's hearts; show which of these two you have chosen.'" **ACTS 1:24**

I'd like to consider myself somewhat well-rounded. I enjoy engaging in a number of activities—building furniture and doing home improvement, I fancy myself an artist of sorts, I'm an amateur barbecue connoisseur, I'm a preacher these days, and (as you can see) I write. But the truth is, I'm not really an expert at any of these. Still, there are other things I'd love to do one day, such as summit Mount Rainier, or even Mount McKinley. One day I'd love to teach music or English at the University of Alabama. However, there's a problem with all these—I'm not qualified! Because I'm old and out of shape, if I tried to climb a 20,000 foot mountain, I'd literally die. As far as teaching at my alma mater, I simply don't have the right education and experience, and I probably never will!

During Jesus' time on earth, there were men who followed Him for the duration of His public ministry. In Mark 1, following Jesus' baptism and temptation in the wilderness, we read that Jesus returned to Galilee, the northern rural region of Israel, and began proclaiming the gospel (v. 14). And at the top of His list of priorities was bringing people alongside Him to partner in accomplishing God's mission in the world. He called Peter and Andrew, James and John, and they immediately submitted to His call on their lives, and they followed Him. When it was all said and done, there were twelve men in Jesus' inner circle in whom He would invest and to whom He would entrust the responsibility of carrying on His mission after He left.

However, it had been prophesied that one of Jesus' closest followers would betray Him. King David had written many generations before, "When he is judged, let him be found guilty, and let his prayer be counted as sin. Let his days be few; let another take over his position" (Ps. 109:7-8). Long before it came to be, God foresaw Judas' betrayal, declared that he would be found guilty, and planned for another follower to take his place among the apostles.

In working to identify the right man for the job, Peter took charge and laid out qualifications for the man who would take Judas' place.

- **A follower of Christ from the time of His baptism:** Shortly after John baptized Jesus, Jesus called His disciples and set out with them by His side to do ministry among the people of Israel. Those who had been with Him throughout this time would have heard His teaching, witnessed His miracles, and demonstrated steadfast devotion through the good and bad times. These were all important for the new would-be apostle.

- **A witness of the resurrected Christ:** The resurrection was central to the message the apostles were to preach in spreading the gospel and establishing the church. It was necessary that the new apostle had confidence in and understanding of Jesus' resurrection.

The eleven agreed on these terms and identified two men who met these qualifications—Joseph and Matthias. But who to choose from among the two, they weren't quite sure. Casting lots was a common Old Testament way of discerning God's will (Lev. 16:8-10; Prov. 16:33). It fact, prior to sending the Holy Spirit, this was one of God's prescribed methods, and this was the way the disciples would choose who to add to their number. But before they did cast the lots, they prayed, "You, Lord, know everyone's hearts; show which of these two you have chosen" (v. 24).

They understood that God knew their hearts. They understood what was taught in Proverbs—"The lot is cast into the lap, but its every decision is from the LORD" (16:33). They understood that God controls all things. Nonetheless, because their choice as to who to add to the apostles was an incredibly weighty decision, one that would affect the gospel being spread to the nations, they prayed that God's wisdom would be made explicitly clear to them.

The Lord chose Matthias. Regarding many of our own decisions, we rely on worldly wisdom, make our choices, and go about our business without giving much thought to what God would have us do. Instead, we should devote ourselves to prayer. We no longer have to leave it up to a roll of the dice, because God has sent His Spirit to guide us. When we live in prayerful dependence upon Him, He will reveal to us His desires for our lives.

How do you express dependence on God's wisdom in your day-to-day life?

How have you seen godly wisdom make a difference in your life, even concerning small decisions?

What's a big decision you'll be making soon? How will you pursue God's help in making sure you walk according to His will?

PRAY WITH JESUS

Father, I recognize that I'm not nearly as wise as I'd like to think I am, and that I desperately need You to guide me in Your wisdom. Help me to make choices that honor You as I seek to live in obedience day by day.

JOURNAL YOUR OWN PRAYER:

"Now if any of you lacks wisdom, he should ask God—who gives to all generously and ungrudgingly—and it will be given to him. But let him ask in faith without doubting. For the doubter is like the surging sea, driven and tossed by the wind. That person should not expect to receive anything from the Lord, being double-minded and unstable in all his ways." **JAMES 1:5-8**

In our world of memes, sarcasm, puns, and social media, being clever is valued just about as much as being genuinely wise. And many times, the number Instagram followers determines influence more than education and experience. Because of this, when we have questions, the first place we often turn is to social media. After all, our platforms now have "recommendations" features, so why not use it, right?

For some questions, the interwebs are a perfectly appropriate resource. For instance, if you're looking for an Einstein bobblehead doll, your best bet is consulting the thousands of online opinions. However, if you're wondering about how to treat the swelling that's mysteriously popped up in your leg, a trip to the doctor is probably in order. Tragically, many people bring not only those sorts of questions, but also those with eternal significance as well. We all know that there are two topics which are off limits when it comes to online etiquette—politics and religion. Nonetheless, social media, blogs, and forums are filled with people ready to offer their opinions about every idea under the sun, and many who are vulnerable naïvely buy in without a second thought.

Many times, Christians' approach isn't too much different from the rest of the world. Sure, we seek godly wisdom for issues that are super spiritual. But for questions of everyday life, we seek the same resources as everyone else. In the preceding verses, James addressed the fact that all people will face trials. In the spiritual sense, we often think of trials as hardships, and this certainly applies. However, it's much more than that. "Trials" refers to the instances which demonstrate our innocence or guilt—faithfulness, or a lack thereof—before the Lord. We are called to live in obedience to God and for His glory, and during hard times, we show how deep our commitment truly is.

Followers of Jesus are called to live with joy at all times, especially when we face hardships. We're able to do this because our hearts are set on eternity, and even though things may not go the way we'd like in the immediate context, we know that in the big picture God is in control and things are going to work out according to His plan. It's not just a positive-attitude-wishful-thinking hoping things will be okay, but a deep-seated trust that God will take care of His children.

No matter who we ask, the world doesn't possess the wisdom to teach us to live this way, nonetheless, we are called to live it out. Therefore, God calls us seek Him continually that we would know moment by moment how we can find joy in the midst of trouble. And here's perhaps the best part—because God is generous and genuinely desires that we would possess His gift of joy, He freely gives it to us when we ask in faith.

There will be times when we're tempted to take our eyes off God and focus on our troubles. Peter experienced something similar (Matt. 14:22-32). In the middle of a storm, he and the other disciples saw Jesus walking on the water. When Jesus called Peter to get out of the boat, in faith, Peter did just that and walked on the water—that is, until he was distracted by the storm. As he began to sink, he called out in desperation and Jesus promptly rescued him. But Peter had to wrestle with a tough question—"You of little faith, why did you doubt?" (Matt. 14:31).

God is happy to carry us through the storms of life, and true joy is available to us if we ask God for it in faith. When we doubt, it's as if we're driven by the same winds that cause the ocean waves. But when we genuinely trust God and continually pursue Him in prayer, He sets us on the stable foundation that allows us to be unshakable through even life's fiercest storms.

When has a storm in life caused you to take your eyes off of Christ?

When have you experienced joy in the middle of hardship that others couldn't understand?

What have you experienced a "trial" in which God found you faithful? How can you leverage these times for the gospel?

PRAY WITH JESUS

Father, I pray that You'd help me to experience true joy, especially during life's trials. I can't understand how to live this way according to worldly wisdom, so I pray You would provide me with heavenly wisdom.

JOURNAL YOUR OWN PRAYER:

"When you pray, don't babble like the Gentiles, since they imagine they'll be heard for their many words. Don't be like them, because your Father knows the things you need before you ask him." **MATTHEW 6:7-8**

I remember when I had to write my first research paper in high school, I thought I'd never be able to come up with five pages of material. Our teacher was kind to teach us how to choose a topic, identify resources at the library (we didn't have the internet since it was the 90s), and how to make sure to avoid plagiarism. Plus, she gave us an entire semester to do the work! So I worked hard, and within a few weeks, I'd put together a paper I was really proud of—and I fulfilled the five-page requirement!

A few years later, my perspective on page requirements was totally different. Whereas before, I thought I'd never be able to write enough—and I was intentional about every word!—by the time I was in college, I'd learned that I could write any length paper with just a few ideas and a lot of fluff! In case you're wondering, fluff is great for a pillow or a puppy, but expanding intellectual ideas without adding any legitimate substance is pretentious and has no value whatsoever.

Christians often take this approach concerning our prayers. We think that if we can turn a phrase or use the right words, God will be more likely to respond to our prayers. Professors, for better or worse, may be impressed with students' capacity to manipulate language in sophisticated ways, but there's no level of intricacy or elegance that can even begin to earn God's admiration. It's not the words of our prayers that move God—it's the heart behind the prayers.

Jesus appealed to the practices of pagan people who prayed to foreign gods. In 1 Kings 18, we read of Elijah's showdown with the prophets of Baal. The respective sides would each pray to their respective deity, and the one to answer would prove to be the true God. In verse 26, we read that the pagan prophets prayed over and over again—literally for hours—"Baal, answer us!" But there was no reply. This can be classified as babbling, and when Jesus uses this term, He referred to the practice of meaninglessly stuttering prayers but with no thought or intentionality behind them. People thought there was value in the quantity of prayers and they had no regard for the quality of prayers.

As a father of six kiddos, you'd better believe I receive plenty of requests from day to day. When my children carelessly ask for something over and over, and over again, this does nothing to move my heart. In fact, my response is often one of annoyance or frustration. However, when one of my little girls crawls up in my lap, bats her eyes, and sweetly asks, "Papa, I'd really appreciate if you'd do this for me," you'd better believe I'm inclined to do whatever she asks. It's not a matter of manipulation, but of heartfelt communication based on a close relational connection.

Jesus taught that prayer should be this way. We're certainly to be persistent in asking for the things we desire and need (Luke 18:1-8). However, the value isn't in the repetition itself, but in the heart behind the asking. When Jesus spent all night praying, His words to the Father weren't a continual flow of mindless drivel, but the genuine expression of a man who wanted continually to be in the presence of His Father.

When we pray, we're to follow the instruction and the model of Jesus. We're to come again and again into God's presence. And it's perfectly appropriate to ask for the same things over and over. But we need to keep in mind that God doesn't honor vain repetition. He knows our needs before we ask, and He knows our hearts as well, and we must come before Him with humility and sincerity.

What have you prayed for over and over again?

Do you feel like your prayers were genuinely honest or have there been times you tend to "babble" as verse 7 says in reference to the Gentiles?

In your own words, how did Jesus pray all night long without babbling and repetition? How can you grow in praying this way?

PRAY WITH JESUS

Father, I confess that there are times when I pray but my heart is not totally in it. Thank You for being patient with me when I'm less than genuine and faithful. Please help me to pray with honesty and humility.

JOURNAL YOUR OWN PRAYER:

Session 4
TO SEE JESUS' GLORY

Focal Passage // Luke 9:18-20,28-29

Memory Verse // John 1:14

The Word became flesh and dwelt among us. We observed his glory, the glory as the one and only Son from the Father, full of grace and truth.

Weekly Reading // Luke 7:1–9:62

Let's be honest. Teenagers like to primp and preen a little more than your average human. From what I hear, it's no big deal for a 16-year-old girl to spend an hour and a half in front of a mirror making sure every blush and shadow, every hair, eyebrow and eyelash are in place. And you guys can't point fingers—with your hair product and body sprays!

What lengths do you go to make sure you come across just right?

We do this because, in our day and time, image is everything! If our bodies are shaped perfectly, we're the envy of all our friends. And if our image isn't right, we're at best ignored, and at worst, shamed by classmates who can be very cruel. If our faces are a beauty to behold, we'll be admired by the masses. But if not, we're tossed aside and seen as insignificant along with the rest of society. It's amazing how much appearance means these days.

In Jesus' day, appearances were pretty important too. The Pharisees dressed to attract attention (Matt. 23:5). After all, they had it all together (or so they thought), and they wanted everyone to know it. On top of their clothing, they would stand in the public squares, praying for all to hear so the crowds would be profoundly impressed by their theological prowess. They were the experts, and they wanted everyone to know it. It was all about appearances.

We see other instances of people dressing to impress in Scripture. Both Paul and Peter addressed the issue of women coming to worship dressed to attract attention to themselves instead of toward the Lord (1 Tim. 2:9-10; 1 Pet. 3:3-4). Jesus, however, approached things differently. Whereas we tend to do everything we can to look as good as possible to others—after all, this helps us to get ahead in this world—Jesus lowered Himself. He took on the "form of a servant" instead of royalty (Phil. 2:7). "He didn't have an impressive form or majesty that we should look at him, no appearance that we should desire him. He was despised and rejected by men" (Isa. 53:2b-3a).

The Jews had for generations longed for their Messiah to arrive. But they had a particular image in mind—and Jesus didn't match it. However, through the way He lived and loved, taught and served, He demonstrated very clearly the character of God. As He spent time with His disciples, they got a first-hand view of these things, but they still had trouble understanding just who Jesus was. So Jesus did for them something truly special—He prayed they would be able to see who He was, and He gave them a clear vision of His glory. We should pray for the same thing today.

Watch this session's video, and then continue to the group discussion section using the content provided.

GROUP DISCUSSION

WHO DO YOU SAY I AM?

Here's a principle that's woven into the fabric of our being—joy we experience is made more full when we share it with others. Luke 9 begins with Jesus sending out His disciples with the authority to minister powerfully to the needs of the people they met. After traveling from village to village, healing the sick, casting out demons, and preaching the good news, they returned to Jesus to share about all they'd experienced. They were excited to say the least, but it's also safe to say they were worn out. So Jesus arranged to have some private time with His followers. He took them to Bethsaida, a small rural town on the northeastern shore of the Sea of Galilee.

However, when the crowds heard that Jesus was there, they chased after Him looking for more of what He had to give. As Jesus commonly did, because He loved people and had compassion on them, He taught and healed. And as if these weren't extraordinary enough, on this occasion He fed thousands with just a few rolls and a couple of small fish.

After all this, though His plans had been set back a bit, Jesus was alone with His disciples and He was praying. This is the first time we see anyone with Jesus as He prayed, and His disciples close by, we see Jesus take a break from communicating with the Father to ask His disciples a question—"Who do the crowds say that I am?" After the disciples answered, Jesus asked them an even more important question: "But you, who do you say that I am?"

The issue of Jesus' identity has been raised throughout His Galilean ministry:
- Luke 4:22—"Isn't this Joseph's son?"
- Luke 5:21—"Who is this man who speaks blasphemies?"
- Luke 7:16—"A great prophet has risen among us"
- Luke 7:49—"Who is this man who even forgives sins?"
- Luke 8:25—"Who then is this? He commands even the winds and the waves ..."

Some of the people who had an encounter with Jesus were way off base, and some were on the right track, but to this point, apart from God's prophet, John the Baptist (John 1:29), no one had a clear understanding of who Jesus was. The enormous crowds that relentlessly pursued Jesus knew there was something different about Him, after all, they'd seen Him do miracles and cast out demons. But they missed the fact that He was God's Messiah.

To this point, the disciples had called Jesus "Rabbi," and respected Him so much that they were willing to make great sacrifices to follow this great teacher. But this wasn't enough. In order to know God the way they needed to, they had to recognize Jesus as the Messiah. So Jesus prayed for them, and He asked them a question. Bold Peter responded for the group, and he responded rightly—we know that You are "God's Messiah."

How do you answer Jesus' question, "Who do you say that I am?"

BACK TO THE MOUNTAIN

The teenage life (and honestly, the human life) is one fraught with conflict. When the alarm goes off at 6 a.m., there's a great internal struggle. Mom says, "Sweetie, make sure you're home by 9:30." At first there's internal conflict (Should I say what I'm thinking or keep my mouth shut?), then there's the potential of a real-world clash between parent and child. And, let's be honest, we don't always see eye-to-eye with our friends, and though we'll definitely hug it out later, we've all had a terrible tussle or two with those we're closest to. Describe a recent time your views clashed with someone you're close to.

Following Peter's confession, Jesus taught the disciples that He must suffer and die, but there was good news. He'd be raised! Further, Jesus shared that those who wished to follow Him—those who would share in His resurrection—must be willing to take up their own cross. This was different than what God's people had understood for generations, so Peter (the man who had just said, "Jesus, we know You're God's Messiah"), because for some reason he thought he knew better, took Jesus aside and corrected Him—"That's not the way it's supposed to work." Jesus' response is one for the ages—"Get behind me, Satan!" (Mark 8:33).

Peter and the disciples had taken steps forward in understanding Jesus' identity. They'd moved from "Teacher" to "Messiah," but they still didn't grasp the full measure of Jesus' identity, and there was not only an outward confrontation between Jesus and Peter—more importantly, their beliefs and perspectives were still at odds. The disciples had come to believe that Jesus was indeed the one who would rescue God's people, but they imagined Jesus' glory as coming by way of His conquering Israel's oppressors. Jesus, however, wanted them to understand that His glory would come through suffering, and they had yet to behold Jesus in His full glory.

Not long before, Jesus had stolen away to a mountain to pray alone. Following these events, Jesus again went to a mountain to pray, but this time He took His three closest followers. As they slept (let's not be too hard on the disciples—they'd been busy doing ministry, and they were worn out!), He would pray, and the answer to His prayers would profoundly impact the disciples' answer to the question, "Who do you say that I am?"

When the disciples awoke, they were amazed to find Jesus keeping company with Moses and Elijah, The great Lawgiver and the great Prophet. These men were so important, in fact, that God buried one (Deut. 34:6) and the other passed to heaven in a chariot of fire (2 Kings 2:1,11), and the disciples respected them immensely. Moses and Elijah, representing the Law and the Prophets, gave testimony that Jesus would accomplish what they never could—He would perfectly fulfill all the law and secure eternal deliverance for God's people.

When have you disagreed with God about what's right and wrong, or about what's true? How did God correct you?

A CHANGE IN APPEARANCE

As they were praying, and as the disciples dozed off, something extraordinary happened. Not only did two of God's great prophets appear alongside Jesus—His appearance actually changed! His face shined like the sun and His clothes even became sparkling white.

The disciples, who were faithful Jews themselves, were undoubtedly familiar with Moses' similar experience found in the Old Testament Scriptures. God's glory and presence was manifest in a variety of ways—as pillars of cloud and fire (Ex. 13:21-22), as a burning bush (Ex. 3:2-4), as fire and smoke, thunder and lightning (Ex. 19:16-18), as a whirlwind (Job 38:1), as well as others. One way God certainly revealed Himself was through light.

When Jesus came to earth, one of His great purposes was to reveal the character of God. In fact, "the entire fullness of God's nature dwells bodily in Christ" (Phil. 2:9)—He's the perfect picture of God's glory! The disciples had walked alongside Jesus as He did ministry, they'd talked endlessly over meals together, and they'd come to recognize Jesus as not only a great teacher, but also as the God who would rescue His people. But they hadn't yet understood the fullness of Jesus' identity.

As Jesus prayed, His glory became fully evident, and when the disciples beheld His transfigured appearance, they understood that this Messiah wasn't some ordinary man who would rescue by earthly means. Jesus was divine and He would deliver God's people in a way only God could devise. The disciples had rejected that Jesus would die and be raised. However, this new revelation certainly played an important role in helping them understand that Jesus' glory would be revealed through His suffering to the point of death, only to be raised victorious over death three days later.

Whereas, because of pride and in order to come across the way we want, we usually try to mask our flaws, Jesus concealed His full identity as an act of humility, and He waited for the right moment to reveal Himself. One day, Jesus' glory will be fully revealed not only to His closest followers, but to all creation. In fact, there will be no sun because Jesus will be all the light we'll need (Rev. 21:23). Of course, we all want to be there, and we want our friends and loved ones to be there as well. In fact, God desires that all people would be there (1 Tim. 2:4). Jesus' prayers no doubt impacted the disciples' understanding of who He was. If we want others to recognize Jesus' true identity, we're called to follow Jesus' example in praying their eyes would be opened.

What is the clearest or most powerful revelation you've ever had concerning the identity of Jesus? How did this impact your life?

1. Who Do You Say I Am?

Before the crowds, Jesus had testified to His nature with signs and wonders. To His disciples, Jesus told them on multiple occasions who He was. However, they missed it. But Jesus prayed, and the eyes of His disciples were opened.

Describe a time you struggled to understand a concept, but then the light came on and your eyes were opened.

How can you communicate the truth about Jesus so that others can come to know Him?

2. Back to the Mountain

In addition to telling His disciples who He was and how He'd rescue God's people, Jesus, because He's gracious and desires that we'd know Him, took His closest followers to the mountain to demonstrate His glory.

When have you had trouble believing the truth about Jesus?

How has the testimony of others impacted your perspectives on life and faith? How has Scripture convinced you of the truth?

3. A Change in Appearance

Jesus took the three disciples to the mountain because He wanted to reveal Himself clearly and unmistakably to them. They not only received the testimony of Moses and Elijah, but they witnessed Jesus' revealing Himself in a powerful way. And what they learned is that, despite their already believing Jesus was the Messiah, He was more glorious than they'd ever have imagined.

How should this statement impact your living?—"When we live like Jesus, God's glory shines through us!"

PRAY LIKE JESUS

Take a few minutes right now to pray for these things. Make it a point to pray:
- That you would have a right and personal knowledge of the glory of Jesus
- That you would be fully convinced by the testimony of Scripture, and that your belief would translate into obedience that glorifies God
- That your heart would be captured by the beauty of Jesus

"Then Moses said, 'Please, let me see your glory.'" **EXODUS 33:18**

When God's people suffered in slavery to the Egyptians, they cried out to God and He heard their groanings with compassion. God's response was to miraculously free His people from their oppressors. As they journeyed to the land that God had promised them, God spoke to Moses with a covenant for His people—if they would follow God in obedience, He would bless them and set them apart as His own special people. The people immediately responded, "Yes, we will do what God has said!"

Moses was up and down the mountain several times, communicating messages between God and the people (Ex. 19:2-8,10,16,20; 20:21; 24:1,9). God called Moses back to the mountain where he would spend 40 days receiving the laws God had for His people. While Moses was away, the Israelites began to wonder what was taking him so long, and they were ready to move along on their journey to the place God had promised. Perhaps they thought some of the following things about Moses.

- **He had died:** Moses had warned the people that entering God's presence was serious business, and that death was the consequence of entering irreverently (Ex. 19:21).

- **He had gone back to Egypt:** The people had complained that it would have been better to stay in Egypt than to wander around in the desert (Ex. 16:3). Maybe Moses thought the same thing and abandoned them.

- **He decided to stay with God on the mountain:** The people had repeatedly complained to Moses (Ex. 14:11-12; 15:24; 16:2). Maybe he'd finally had enough, and decided to stay with God.

Either way, they didn't know what had come of their leader, and they were ready to move along. But they didn't want to do so without a visible god to go before them. So they convinced Aaron to fashion for them an idol. Aaron then built an altar and organized a festival at which the people worshiped the calf and celebrated that they would move on to the home God had promised.

God was appalled by the people's unfaithfulness, and in His anger threatened to destroy them. But Moses pleaded on their behalf, "Turn from your fierce anger and relent concerning this disaster planned for your people" (Ex. 32:12b). After all, God had promised to bless them—what would other nations think if God abandoned them now? So God relented, and communicated to Moses that the people were free to move on. However, God would no longer be with them.

Moses simply couldn't accept this. He knew the Lord by name, and God knew Moses personally and was pleased with him. It was unimaginable that he would lose his relationship with God, and for Moses, he'd rather have stayed in the desert with God than to move on to a place that had it all, but without God. God's response to Moses— "My presence will go with you, and I will give you rest" (v. 14).

Moses had as intimate a relationship with God as any man has ever enjoyed this side of heaven (apart from Jesus). He had met with God time and time again on the mountain. He had seen God perform incredible miracles. He had followed God as He led by pillars of cloud and fire. Moses' connection with the Lord was special, but he wanted more. So he asked God, "Please, let me see your glory" (Ex. 33:18).

For many Christians today, we're quite familiar with God, and religion can become routine. The singing, praying, Bible reading, and church-going can become so commonplace that we lose our hunger for the things of God. However, when our faith seems ordinary, we're missing out on the infinite nature of God who's happy to reveal Himself to us—if we'd only ask. Because of Moses' hunger for God, and his refusal to be satisfied with anything apart from God, when he made his request of the Lord, He gladly granted what Moses asked.

Today, we need to ask ourselves, how hungry are we to experience the glory of God? When we refuse to be satisfied with anything else, we can be confident that God will reveal Himself to us.

What things bring you satisfaction but hinder your desire for God?

What are some ways we, like the Israelites, turn from God to pursue "idols" in our lives?

What can you learn from Moses about cultivating the desire to know God?

PRAY WITH JESUS

Father, I confess that there are times I'm unfaithful to You and I pursue the idols of the world. Thank You for Your willingness to be patient and to forgive. Help me to hunger more and more for You. Please, God, show me Your glory.

JOURNAL YOUR OWN PRAYER:

DEVO // DAY 2

"The heavens declare the glory of God, and the expanse proclaims the work of his hands."
PSALM 19:1

I grew up in a family that was really close. My dad coached my baseball teams growing up, and my mom spent time volunteering in my elementary classrooms. On the weekends, my parents would take my friends and me to the lake, or to the movies, or out to eat. My family consisted of great relationships, and the foundation for this was:

- Our time together
- Good communication

I have great memories of sitting in the living room with my family, and doing what people don't do nearly enough these days—talking. The TV wasn't on, and we weren't listening to music, scrolling through our social media feeds, or playing games on our phones (we didn't even have smart phones then). We were simply sharing about the things we cared about. It wasn't all super important stuff, though sometimes it certainly was. It was just a matter of sharing the things we cared about.

This kind of sharing is how we knew one another so well, but there were other kinds of communication too. For instance, we lived in a rural part of Alabama, and fishing was one of my favorite pastimes. And it just so happened that there were seven ponds and a large creek within walking distance from our house. During the summers, I'd leave the house about as early as the sun came up, and my parents wouldn't see me until either I was hungry, or until they called me. Remember, this was the days before everybody had a phone in their pocket, so my parents had a special way of calling me home. The house we lived in had a large church bell in the yard (where it came from, I have no idea), and when we rang it, it could be heard literally for miles. That was a good thing, because sometimes I would be miles away. And when I heard the bell ring, I knew what it meant—time to come home!

God communicates to us in multiple ways. Primarily, the way we are able to know Him personally and understand the details of His character and His ways, is communicated through His Word. He also communicates through His world. In Psalm 19:1, we read that "the heavens declare the glory of God, and the expanse proclaims the work of his hands." Through creation, we don't know enough to build a relationship with God. We don't understand the details about Jesus and the Holy Spirit. There's no way for us to understand faith and forgiveness, repentance and obedience. However, creation does send a powerful message that we simply can't ignore. The works of God's hands declare clearly that God is real, He is powerful and wise, and He is glorious!

All that we see exists by the power of God, and there's no other way it could have been. If we have hearts set on experiencing the glory of God, we should pay attention to the heavens. When seen rightly through the truths of Scripture, there's a powerful message about His glory.

When has creation helped you to appreciate something about God's glory?

How do the heavens—the skies, the sun, moon, and stars, outer space—proclaim the glory of God?

How do you think God would like to use you to declare His glory so that others could hear about Him?

PRAY WITH JESUS

Father, thank You for the ways You communicate with your people. I pray that You would help me to have eyes to see and ears to hear all the things that You want to communicate to me. Help me, in turn, to communicate Your glory to others.

JOURNAL YOUR OWN PRAYER:

"Staring at him in awe, he said, 'What is it, Lord?' The angel told him, 'Your prayers and your acts of charity have ascended as a memorial offering before God.'" **ACTS 10:4**

Every Mother's Day, we all buy our mom flowers and a card, we give her a hug or a call, and express how much we love and appreciate her (at least you'd better!). Consider this scenario. On the special day set aside to honor your mom, you wake up late and stroll into lunch, and you hadn't even thought about her. Upon your dad's asking, "Hey kiddo, what did you get for mom—don't you know it's Mother's Day?," you run to your room and promptly return with a sloppy "handmade" card you've created just for her. But she knows you forgot. How do you think it would make your mom feel?

Many Jews throughout history followed all the practices prescribed by their religion. However, it's not the mere actions that please God. Isaiah brought an accusation against the people— "These people approach me with their speeches to honor me with lip-service—yet their hearts are far from me, and human rules direct their worship of me" (29:13). Jesus brought the same charge against Israel's religious leaders, "This people honors me with their lips, but their heart is far from me. They worship me in vain, teaching as doctrines human commands" (Matt. 15:8-9). Many of Israel's people pursued all the right things, but their hearts weren't in it. Therefore, God rejected their cheap attempts at worship. God might have felt like your mom would have, knowing your gift was out of obligation and not heartfelt.

Cornelius was a centurion who lived in Caesarea and worked among Jewish people. Though he was a Roman, Cornelius was a worshiper of the true God, and had converted to Judaism. He was well respected by the Jewish community, and as the Bible teaches, he was very kind to the Jewish people. As a worshiper who was faithful to what the religion required, Cornelius gladly offered daily prayers to the Lord. However, unlike many, he didn't do it out of obligation. His acts of kindness and his prayers flowed from a genuine love for and desire to know God.

One day, as he was praying, Cornelius had a vision of an angel who had a message for him—"Your prayers and your acts of charity have ascended as a memorial offering before God." God had revealed Himself to Cornelius, but now He was about to reveal His glory more fullly to this faithful worshiper. The angel instructed Cornelius to send for Peter, and at the same time God was working in Cornelius' life, He was at work in Peter.

To this point, Peter knew it was unlawful for a Jewish man to visit with "unclean" Gentiles. However, as one of Christ's apostles who understood clearly the message of the gospel and who was charged with taking that message to the world, God had revealed to Peter that he was responsible to deliver the good news to Cornelius and his family. Peter preached the truth about Jesus, and the Holy Spirit came down, they worshiped God, and were baptized.

Cornelius had devoted himself to loving God and people. Further, he was a man devoted to prayer. As he pursued a relationship with Lord, God used Peter to reveal to Cornelius a fuller picture of the glory of Jesus. Most of us won't have a vision of an angel. We won't have an apostle seek us out in order to preach the gospel. But we have something just as good, or better! God has come to us through His Word and through His church with the gospel. He's calling us day by day to seek Him just as Cornelius did. And when we devote ourselves to worship and prayer, we can be sure God will reveal His glory to us.

When have you served God out of obligation and not from the heart?

What helps you make sure your worship is genuine?

How do you live in order to put yourself in the position, like Cornelius, to see God's glory?

PRAY WITH JESUS

Father, I understand that my sin separated me from You, and that I had no part among Your people. However, You came to me with the message of Jesus and offered the gift of salvation. Thank you for revealing Your glory to me.

JOURNAL YOUR OWN PRAYER:

"I pray that the eyes of your heart may be enlightened in order that you may know the hope to which he has called you, the riches of his glorious inheritance in his holy people."
EPHESIANS 1:18

When God established a covenant people, He promised to set them apart as His special people, and to allow them to live in relationship with Him—they only needed to live in obedience to His commands (Ex. 19:3-6). Later, God would communicate further that, if they obeyed God's law, He would bless them. However, if they failed to follow God's desires for His people, they would receive curses instead (Deut. 11:26-28). We see this principle in our lives today. For instance, when we obey the law, we enjoy the many freedoms available to us. But when a sixteen-year-old decides to have a little fun with dad's car, and decides to ignore the speed limit, he forfeits blessings which were available had he only followed the rules. He also invites consequences from the law—and from mom and dad (can anyone say grounded!).

After a brief greeting, Paul opens his letter to the Ephesian church with this statement— "Blessed is the God and Father of our Lord Jesus Christ, who has blessed us with every spiritual blessing in the heavens in Christ" (1:3). What an amazing thought! We have "every" blessing we need:

- **We are chosen:** Before He established the world, God chose us to be the instruments of His glory, and it brings Him pleasure to bring us into His family.

- **We are redeemed:** By our rebellion against God, we sold ourselves into slavery to sin. But Jesus paid the price to buy us out of bondage so that we could live in freedom.

- **We have an inheritance:** Jesus is the heir of "all things" (Heb. 1:2) and He has chosen to share His inheritance with us (Rom. 8:17). That Jesus has inherited a name above all names (Heb. 1:4) represents His power and authority over all creation. That we share in His inheritance means we will rule alongside Him for eternity.

- **We are sealed:** When we come to faith in Christ, the Holy Spirit comes into our lives, and secures us at that moment for eternity.

These blessings are absolutely amazing and are promised to every person who comes to faith in Christ. However, the same conditions apply today (although in a different way) that God set forth in Deuteronomy. God's blessings are available to those who are righteous— those who live in obedience to His laws. However, there's a problem. God's standard is perfect obedience, and there's no person who can live up to that standard. What this means, quite frankly, is that God's blessings are simply out of reach.

However, all along God knew we'd never be able to live up to the requirements, so He sent Jesus in our place, who lived in full obedience and perfectly fulfilled the law's requirements.

Jesus took upon Himself the curse for our sin, and when we are "in Christ," we instead receive the blessings for His obedience.

For this to be a reality in our lives, we must have a vision of the glory of Jesus—we must have our eyes opened to see who He truly is. This is where prayer comes in—apart from the Holy Spirit's opening our eyes, we are totally blind to spiritual things. We should continually pray for ourselves and others that God would help us to receive this first gift of having our hearts enlightened, that we would in turn, but the life and sacrifice of Jesus, be in the position to receive all the other blessings He gives to His people.

What are the greatest blessings God has given you?

In your own words, why are you in the position to receive blessings from the Lord?

Why is seeing Jesus clearly one of the greatest blessings available to us?

PRAY WITH JESUS

Father, thank You for all the blessings that are made available to me in Christ. I understand that it's only through Him that I have access to these spiritual blessings, and I pray that You'd help me to see Christ clearly every day so that I can live for Your glory.

JOURNAL YOUR OWN PRAYER:

"Now my soul is troubled. What should I say—Father, save me from this hour? But that is why I came to this hour. Father, glorify your name." Then a voice came from heaven: "I have glorified it, and I will glorify it again." **JOHN 12:27-28**

We all want to be successful. If we pride ourselves on being a good student, we want to make good grades. If we're into music, we want to play or sing well. If sports is our thing, we want to accomplish great things. We pursue success for several reasons. For one, we all have a job to do, and when we're talking about vocation, greater success translates into greater pay. In many ways, this means we have the things we need and the opportunity to use what God gives to influence others. However, money is not the only reason we desire success. The student who makes an A+ receives no pay for studying so hard, nonetheless, there's great satisfaction. This is because we were designed to desire the good-jobs and well-dones from those in positions of authority, and even from our peers. So many young people want to be athletes and movie stars not only because of the big contracts, but also because of the glory.

The term *glory* has several specific meanings.

- **Light:** When Moses was on the mountain and asked to see the Lord's glory, God allowed it. When Moses came down to the people, the people were afraid of him because he was glowing—he'd been in the presence of the Lord's glory. When Jesus invited three of His disciples to join Him on the mountain and was transfigured before them, He began literally to shine in their presence—His glory was made evident through radiant light (Luke 9:28-29). When we were lost in darkness, Jesus, the Light of the world, allowed us to see the truth.

- **Fame:** The psalms teach us that the Lord will rule in righteousness throughout all eternity. Therefore, His fame will spread to all people throughout all generations (102:12). During His time on earth, Jesus preached about the kingdom of God to thousands upon thousands. We, likewise, are called to tell of the Lord's greatness to anyone who would listen. When we speak of God's name, we glorify Him by spreading His fame.

- **Weight:** Ultimately, glory means shining light on and spreading the fame of the name of God. In the Bible, a name is much more than a label. Someone's name is representative of who they are, and God's name represents the fullness of His character—loving, just, kind, generous, gracious, faithful, and so much more. God's name isn't something we should take lightly. To the contrary, His name is substantial—weighty—and we glorify Him by helping others to know His character.

We've been made to desire glory. However, if we understand this only as being famous within our culture, we're mistaken. We've taken the idea of glory and corrupted it in the sense that most people today desire fame to feed their pride. However, rightly pursued, it refers not to being known by the masses, but being known by God. To be open, transparent, and fully known before God is one of the most satisfying—and humbling—experiences available to us.

While Jesus was on earth, He was quite famous. We read in Luke, "But the news about him spread even more, and large crowds would come together to hear him and to be healed of their sicknesses" (5:15). Surely He found some satisfaction in this, right? After all, we certainly would. However, Jesus wasn't here for His own glory. Everything He pursued was for the sake of glorifying the Father. Jesus knew that meant going to the cross, and even though He desperately wanted to avoid the pain—not just in a physical sense, but the emotional and spiritual pain associated with taking on our sin and being separated from the Father—He willingly obeyed.

We are called to the same broad purpose as Jesus—to glorify God with our lives. There may be times when we'd like to do things a little differently than what God has called us to. However, when our ultimate desire is to honor God, we'll say like Jesus, "What should I say— Father, save me from this hour? But that is why I came to this hour. Father, glorify your name."

When have your desires failed to line up with God's desires for you?

What is God calling you to at this time in your life in order to bring Him glory?

What would God have you sacrifice in order to help others to see His goodness?

PRAY WITH JESUS

Father, I confess that there are times when the things I desire aren't in line with Your standards and Your will. Help me to desire Your glory above all other things, and to be willing to give up the things I want in order to honor You.

JOURNAL YOUR OWN PRAYER:

Session 5
ONLY THROUGH JESUS

Focal Passage // Luke 10:21-22; 11:1-4

Memory Verse // John 14:6
*Jesus told him, "I am the way, the truth, and the life.
No one comes to the Father except through me."*

Weekly Reading // Luke 10:1-15:32

When I was in elementary school, when asked what I wanted to be when I grow up, I'd say enthusiastically, *I want to play third base for the Yankees!* I was a baseball fanatic—not a fan just in the sense that I liked to watch, but an enthusiast in every sense. By the time I was in high school, my older cousin was playing college baseball, and no matter how hard I worked or how much talent I had, my puny ninth grade body just couldn't hit, throw, or run like a legitimate college athlete. I remember asking him over and over, "how do you do that?!"

What's something you've seen someone else do that you want desperately to be able to do yourself?

When Jesus came on the scene, there had been no such message in quite a long time. The Jews were experiencing oppression at the hands of the Roman empire, and the last time they'd heard from God was through the prophet Malachi over 400 years ago, and His message wasn't exactly encouraging—*I have loved you, yet you have profaned my altar, you've stolen from me, you've been adulterous!* The Jews knew from experience that these sorts of charges were accompanied by harsh consequences, and this time was no exception. As time passed, God's people came to realize they were suffering perhaps the worst punishment imaginable—for hundreds of years, they'd received no word from the Lord, and they probably wondered, *have we finally gone too far? Has God forsaken us?*

The Pharisees taught that one needed only follow the law in order to earn God's favor, but this sort of religion was lifeless—a heavy weight to bear instead of a divine relationship that lifts us out of life's brokenness. Prior to following Jesus, the disciples had taken part in this sterile routine which was their religion, but they knew something was missing. But with Jesus, something was different. When they observed Him praying, they recognized He had a connection with the Father like they'd never seen before. *He knows something we don't. Maybe He's received a message from God!*

God's people longed for a real connection with God. They wanted to be freed from Roman oppression. They wanted to hear from Him. Deep down, we all do, because we were created for a relationship with God. Jesus had in a very real way the things they wanted—a genuine connection with God. So a few, His disciples, followed this great Teacher, and they asked, *will you teach us to connect with God?*

Watch this session's video, and then continue to the group discussion section using the content provided.

REASON TO REJOICE

As a young teenager, I loved (I mean LOVED) guitar music. There was something about a guitar solo that affected me in ways I simply couldn't put into words, and I wanted to be able to do that! However, I thought it was impossible for me, and that someone had to be superhuman to make a guitar truly sing—great guitarists were called "heroes" for a reason. Fast forward a few years, I got a guitar when I went to college, and it wasn't long before I had the opportunity to play in a band. I learned a good lesson real quick—daydreaming about being on stage like the guitar greats and actually making it happen are two totally different things! Sure, I thought I sounded great in my dorm room, but with the band and before a crowd, it was a drastically different story.

Jesus' purpose was never to accomplish all God's purposes on His own. Before we get carried away, let me explain this. There is absolutely nothing we can do about our sin problem. We can work to live a good life, we can go to church, read the Bible, pray, and we can love others—even sacrificially—but none of these even comes close to paying the debt we owed for our sin. Only Jesus could pay that price, and there was never anything anyone else could do to help. Jesus did that alone. However, God's plan all along was to involve Jesus' followers in accomplishing His plans.

As more and more people began following Jesus—not just for the miracles, but those who were truly devoted to Him—He assigned to them a pretty big responsibility. Jesus sent seventy-two of His followers "... ahead of him in pairs to every town and place where he himself was about to go. He told them, 'The harvest is abundant, but the workers are few. Therefore, pray to the Lord of the harvest to send out workers into his harvest. Now go; I'm sending you out like lambs among wolves'" (Luke 10:1b-3). Their job was simple—do the things they'd seen Jesus doing.

This may seem impossible—after all, Jesus had been healing the sick, casting out demons, multiplying food, exercising authority over nature—He'd even raised the dead! However, when Jesus sent them out, He sent them with the authority to do miracles. As they returned from their adventures, they shared that they'd actually been able do the things Jesus told them to do. There were exhilarated! Sure, it was incredible that they'd been able to heal the sick and cast out demons—they were called to live like Jesus, and they were actually following in His ways. But this was by no means the most important thing. In addressing His followers, Jesus reminded them that their relationship with God was more valuable than even these powers.

Then Jesus turned His attention to the Father and prayed—"I praise you, Father...". Jesus knew of the Father's plan to include His followers in impacting the world, and it was happening!

KNOWN THROUGH THE SON

Up until this point, in Jesus' prayers recorded in Luke, we see instances when He prayed, but we don't know details about the content. However, this time it was different. Luke recorded exactly what Jesus prayed, and included is a list of reasons Jesus praised the Father.

- **Lord of all:** Jesus addressed the Father as "Lord of heaven and earth." God is sovereign, and He is in control of all that happens on the earth as well as in the spiritual realm. His plans will be accomplished, and for those who are His children, we will share in His blessings for eternity.

- **Hidden and Revealed:** The Pharisees were seen as the experts, and despite that they knew the Scriptures, they missed out on God's purposes and failed to recognize Jesus as the Messiah. Instead of revealing Himself to the worldly, God chose to open the eyes of people who were humble and helpless from an earthly perspective. Those who thought they were closest to God were, in fact, completely cut off.

- **Entrusted to Jesus:** No one can know God unless Jesus makes Him known to us. This is a great responsibility that has been entrusted to Jesus. Under the old covenant, priests had the great privilege of serving in the tabernacle and temple, and of teaching the law. Only the high priest, who was the supreme religious leader of the Israelites, could enter the most holy place where the presence of God dwelt. And even then, he could only enter once a year. This ministry pointed forward to Jesus, who is our perfect High Priest (Heb. 4:14). Jesus praised God that, through His relationship with the Father, we could have a relationship with God.

Prayer is the act of our going to God in worship, confession of sin, thanksgiving, and in expressing dependence upon Him. However, Scripture teaches that God is so holy, He cannot even look upon sin (Hab. 1:13). Further, if we accept sin in our lives instead of continually turning away, the Lord doesn't even hear our prayers (Ps. 66:18). In fact, in order to approach God, He requires that we are perfect—and none of us are. But Jesus is!

As Jesus celebrated the experiences of His disciples, He recognized that God's purposes were being realized, and His natural response was to offer praise and thanks to God. Jesus has a relationship with the Father the way God intended for all people, and for those who trust in Jesus, we have the privilege of approaching God, not just once a year like the earthly high priests, but any time we choose. Jesus did everything necessary for us to come to God. Let's never neglect this privilege.

How should knowing we approach God only through Jesus affect how we pray?

JESUS' MODEL PRAYER

The disciples followed Jesus because they recognized there was something different about Him, and they came to realize His prayer life was a big part of that difference. So they asked Jesus, *won't you teach us to pray like you pray?*

Jesus' reply is now the most familiar prayer in the world—what we call The Lord's Prayer. However, it contains the request for forgiveness, and we all know Jesus never sinned, so a better way of referring to it may be a Model Prayer which Jesus used as an outline for teaching His followers. These are the ideas we should focus on in our prayers:

- **Praise:** God is holy, and although it doesn't have to be the first thing we do when we pray, we are called to make a priority of recognizing and expressing the worth of God's name and character.

- **Purposes:** God's kingdom is present wherever Jesus reigns. We are to pray that sin and its consequences would be abolished, and instead that people would live in submission to Jesus and according to His purposes. Further, we are to be active in bringing these things about.

- **Provision:** Many times, we think we have the things we need because we work for them. But the truth is we depend on God for everything, even the simplest things. Everything in the universe belongs to God, and we have only what He chooses to give us, and we are called to continually express our dependence on Him.

- **Pardon:** We've all sinned. In fact, because we struggle with the flesh as long as we're in this life, we continue to sin. When we do, we're responsible to ask God for forgiveness—not just generally, but for every specific sin. When we confess and turn away, God is kind to offer forgiveness for sins both big and small, and we're called to forgive in the same way.

- **Protection:** We're caught up in a spiritual battle, and the souls of all people—including our own—are on the line. Because our flesh is weak and tempted toward sin, we need God's strength and protection against the forces of evil which are set on our destruction.

The Pharisees were known for going on and on with elaborate prayers to impress others, but they failed to honestly communicate their hearts. Sometimes, we make prayer more complicated than it actually is. If we make it a point to pray honestly and according to these five points Jesus taught, we will come to find we have a powerful prayer life.

Jesus prayed. Jesus modeled prayer. Jesus taught prayer. And Jesus is the Priest through whom we're connected with God in prayer. Prayer begins and ends with Jesus. If we want to be like Him, it makes sense that we should pray.

1. Reason to Rejoice

Jesus sent His disciples with the capacity to proclaim the gospel with authority and to demonstrate power over demons. Today, it may look different, but when we share the truth of Jesus, the power of God's truth has the power to conquer darkness in the lives of others.

When have you seen the gospel overcome someone's unbelief?

When you share the gospel, you do so by the power and authority of Jesus. How should this impact the way you relate to others?

2. Known Through the Son

The religious leaders of Jesus' day thought that, because they followed the finer points of the law, God was pleased with them and they were close to Him. However, Jesus clearly communicated that we can never approach God based on our merit. We can come to God only by humbly receiving the gospel, turning from our sin, and living in faithful obedience.

How have you, at times, had an attitude like the Pharisees?

In your own words, why are you fit to come into the presence of God?

3. Jesus' Model Prayer

Jesus was different, and it was plain to see. Because the message He preached was offensive, many rejected Him, but a few with humble hearts followed, and they wanted to be like Him. Because prayer was central to Jesus' life, they knew that to be like Jesus meant to pray like Him, so they asked Him to help them learn.

What about your prayer life needs to change in order for you to be more like Jesus?

From the five points outlined, how are you praying well? How do you need to grow? How will improving affect your relationship with God?

PRAY LIKE JESUS

Take a few minutes right now to pray for these things. Make it a point to pray:
- That God would use you to reach people with the gospel
- That God would align your desires to the heart of Christ, so that when you pray, you are truly doing so in Jesus' name
- That you would grow not only in praying like Jesus, but living like Him

"As for me, I vow that I will not sin against the LORD by ceasing to pray for you. I will teach you the good and right way." **1 SAMUEL 12:23**

God called Israel to be His own special people, and He made them a promise—if they listened to God and lived according to His covenant with them, He'd bless them in unimaginable ways. Because of this, Israel was different than every other nation on earth, and the form of government God established was that His people would be led by prophets and priests.

However, time and time again, from the time God delivered Israel from slavery in Egypt, they rejected God and turned aside to idols. Rather than living in continual gratitude for all the ways God blessed them, the Israelites desired the things of foreign nations, including their political system. Up to this point, they'd relied on God to fight for them—to defend them when they were vulnerable and to provide the lands He'd promised to them. However, this wasn't the way all the other nations did it. They had powerful leaders who built strong armies, and who fought by force and not by faith—and this is what the Israelites wanted.

Samuel was a great prophet who served God's people humbly and boldly. However, as he aged, the Israelites saw this as an opportunity to install a new form of government. They asked Samuel to appoint a king (1 Sam. 8:5). Samuel knew this was wrong, and he took his concern to God. God's response was *it's not you they're rejecting ... it's me*! Samuel warned the people of the dangers of rejecting God and committing their lives to the service of a king. However, they ignored all he said, insisting that he give them a king. So he did.

After anointing Saul as king, Samuel gave one final address to the people of Israel. He confronted them with the fact that, by demanding a king, they had rejected God. But he reminded them that, if they would turn away from worthless things and turn their hearts to God, He would bless them—"The LORD will not abandon his people, because of his great name and because he has determined to make you his own people" (1 Sam. 12:22).

Then Samuel made a promise to the people. "As for me, I vow that I will not sin against the LORD by ceasing to pray for you. I will teach you the good and right way" (1 Sam. 12:23).

God had placed into Samuel's hands the responsibility to lead and serve the Israelites. Despite their rejection of his leadership, Samuel wasn't relieved from the responsibility of influencing them to follow God. And that responsibility meant not only confronting them with the truth and reminding them of God's goodness, but also praying unceasingly for their hearts to be softened to God.

For us today, we are called to the same things. We're surrounded by people who have rejected God, and who choose day by day to devote themselves to worthless things. We are called to confront the lies they've bought into, and to warn them of the consequences of their empty pursuits. Further, we are to remind them that, if they choose to turn away from their sinful lifestyle, God is ready and waiting to receive them into His family.

There's power in the truth of God's Word, and when we share it with others, God uses it to change their lives. However, we need to recognize there's nothing we can do to soften hard hearts—that's totally in God's hands. This is why it so important that we continually pray that God would work in the lives of the people we share with. Samuel acknowledged it would have been sin if he'd failed to pray. We need to take prayer that seriously, as well. We need not only share the gospel, but we need to understand that our prayers make a difference in how others will receive what we share. Let's take seriously God's call on our lives to pray for others.

What do people serve as king of their lives in our culture?

What blessings do people miss out on because they've rejected God as King?

What difference does it make when you pray that people would submit to God?

PRAY WITH JESUS

Father, thank You for your willingness to lead your people. God, I confess that there are times when I don't submit to You as the ruler of my life. Please help me to turn away from pursuing worldly things and to turn my heart to You.

JOURNAL YOUR OWN PRAYER:

"I cried out to him with my mouth, and praise was on my tongue. If I had been aware of malice in my heart, the Lord would not have listened. However, God has listened; he has paid attention to the sound of my prayer. Blessed be God! He has not turned away my prayer or turned his faithful love from me." **PSALM 66:17-20**

Many people see middle school as some of the toughest years of their lives. Classes get more complicated, bullying intensifies during this time, and students engage more heavily in social media, where people are even less inclined to hold back on mean words. However, for me, I loved middle school, except for seventh grade math! For one, math was my absolutely least favorite subject, and to make matters worse, my teacher wasn't known to be particularly helpful. On one occasion, I had a question about a new skill we were learning, so naturally, I raised my hand. My teacher looked up and shook her head from side to side. I kept it raised. Again, head shake, but this time with a little more forcefully and with a bit of a scowl. After having my hand in the air for about five minutes and with three or four more increasingly aggressive head shakes, I timidly asked, "Uh, excuse me, Miss Teacher. Can you ..." then she cut in—"Mr. Belcher! That will be one thousand sentences for you. Now be quiet!"

Shut down! She'd made it clear I was not allowed into her space—physically, visually, aurally, or otherwise. She was busy reading her magazine.

God, on the other hand, has invited us to come continually into His presence. If we have questions, we should ask Him. If we have concerns, bring them to Him. He cares for us, and He desires that we bring before Him all the things we care about (1 Pet. 5:7). However, sometimes we may take these ideas as if we can come to God any way we please, and on our own terms. This simply isn't the case.

In the Old Testament, God made it very clear that approaching Him was something to be pursued with the greatest of care. First, not just anyone could come into God's presence. It was a privilege reserved for only priests. Further, before even these few could come before God, they had to take part in elaborate ceremonial cleansing. And if they hadn't followed the prescription perfectly, they risked death. As a tragic example, Nadab and Abihu, who were Aaron's sons, approached the Lord in a way that was unauthorized, and they were consumed by the fire from the altar (Lev. 10:1-2). Coming before God is serious business.

Many times, we may think that because we live under the new covenant, things are altogether different and we no longer need to concern ourselves with these things. It's true that we no longer rely on priests to approach God on our behalf, we don't participate in ceremonial cleansings to approach God, and we don't offer animal sacrifices on an altar. However, it's not because God has done away with the law, but because Christ perfectly fulfilled the things God requires of us.

Though we're no longer required to participate in these external rituals, we're required nonetheless to approach God in the same spirit. Just as God rejected the unauthorized worship of Nadab and Abihu, if we harbor sin in our hearts, God rejects our prayers. Jesus modeled for us in His model prayer (Luke 11:1-4) that we are to pray for God's will to be done. Our hearts are to be set on the realities of God's kingdom becoming reality among us. However, there are times when we'd rather build our own kingdoms that God's.

When our prayers express selfish, sinful desires which are contrary to God's, the Lord doesn't listen to those prayers. However, when we pray with humility, asking that God would conform our desires to His, and that, even through the specific things we ask for, His will would be accomplished, He's happy to hear.

Ultimately, we're accepted into God's presence only through Jesus. Our righteousness could never come close to meeting God's standard. However, when we live by faith in Christ, God invites us into His presence, and He hears our prayers.

Describe a time you've wanted someone's attention, but you were rejected.

In your own words, what determines our being accepted versus rejected by God?

How should it affect your prayer life to know that, when we live by faith in Christ, God "has not turned away my prayer or turned his faithful love from me"?

PRAY WITH JESUS

Father, I've experienced the pain of rejection in my life. I'm thankful that You're ready and willing to receive me into Your presence when I come through Jesus. That You would hear my prayers is an incredible privilege. Help me to approach You in humility and reverence.

JOURNAL YOUR OWN PRAYER:

"Now Peter and John were going up to the temple for the time of prayer at three in the afternoon." **ACTS 3:1**

Jewish law required God's people to participate in three daily prayer times: 9 a.m., noon, and 3 p.m. Tradition holds that this custom was introduced by the patriarchs—Abraham introduced morning prayers, Isaac added prayer in the afternoon, and Jacob added evening prayers,[1] and for generations, the Jewish people recognized the importance of living in prayerful dependence upon God.

Peter and John were no doubt accustomed to this practice. However, because they had come to know Jesus as the Messiah and had devoted their lives to following Jesus, they understood there was a difference between the Jews' habitual practice of daily prayer and the significance of praying through Jesus as their High Priest.

Instead of praying in private, because the Feast of Weeks was an important week in the life of the Jews, Peter and John joined the many worshipers who were going to the temple to worship and pray. But the followers of Jesus had different reasons for going. Whereas the crowds came to the temple out of obligation—the law required that they participated in the festival and offered sacrifices at the temple. Peter and John identified this as the perfect opportunity not only to offer the prayers to God, but also to share the good news of Jesus with people who were waiting for the Messiah.

Just weeks before, as Jesus had entered Jerusalem, the crowds had cried out, "Hosanna to the Son of David! Blessed is he who comes in the name of the Lord!" (Matt. 21:9b). They had believed that Jesus was, at the very least, a prophet sent from God. And this was no small thing—the people of Israel had gone 400 years without even one word from the Lord. However, many thought that Jesus may really be the Messiah that God had promised long ago.

But then Jesus died.

The hope that had swelled in the hearts of so many was dashed, and they were left to go on waiting. Who knows, they thought, maybe we'll be left to suffer under Roman oppression for another 400 years?

However, God's plans had all along been different—and better—than what the Jews expected. When Jesus died, the disciples were as devastated as anyone. Yet, only a few days later, Jesus came to them and presented them with a clear picture of what He'd told them several times before—the nature of the Messiah is not to conquer as a political or military leader, but through service and sacrifice. Even to the point of dying on a cross. However, because Jesus was no ordinary man, and because He has power over sin and death, the grave could not hold Him and He rose from the dead.

This was a message the disciples wanted their Jewish brothers and sisters to hear. They'd missed it, but Jesus made it clear to them. Their fellow worshipers had likewise missed the truth, but Jesus had passed on to His followers the responsibility of sharing the good news with everyone. They were at the temple to pray. But because they were surrounded by people who wanted to know God, but who were going about it the wrong way, Peter and John were there to share the truth of Jesus. God gave them just the opportunity they were looking for, and He used these men to show many people the power and goodness of God.

As we devote ourselves to prayer, we need to be continually aware of opportunities to share about Jesus. We need to pray that God would open doors for the gospel and that He would go before us, preparing the hearts of those who will hear. When we make this a lifestyle, God will use us, just like the disciples, to make a difference in people's lives.

What value is found in practicing prayer as a discipline?

What regular disciplines do you practice in regard to prayer?

How would God have you grow not only in praying, but also in praying specifically for the lost? In sharing with non-believers?

PRAY WITH JESUS

Father, I understand that You've called me to pray regularly and continually. However, there are many times when I don't pray like I should. Help me to pray not as a matter of obligation, but because I long for a continual connection with You.

JOURNAL YOUR OWN PRAYER:

"Therefore, since we have a great high priest who has passed through the heavens—Jesus the Son of God—let us hold fast to our confession. For we do not have a high priest who is unable to sympathize with our weaknesses, but one who has been tempted in every way as we are, yet without sin. Therefore, let us approach the throne of grace with boldness, so that we may receive mercy and find grace to help us in time of need." **HEBREWS 4:14-16**

God is different than we are. There's the understatement of the century, right? God is so different, in fact, that it's difficult to come up with the language to adequately communicate this concept. We might use words like *transcendent, far above, unfathomable, infinite,* or *supreme*. But all these fall short somehow. The truth is that God is altogether different, and we'll never fully grasp that. Jesus is fully God. In fact, for our sins to be forgiven, it was necessary that a sacrifice be offered which was totally pure, innocent, and righteous. Only Jesus could fulfill this requirement.

We need not only a sacrifice for sin, but also a high priest to go before God on our behalf. According to the Old Testament law, only the high priest was allowed into the presence of God. The common people were allowed to come into the inner court, where sacrifices were offered, but they certainly couldn't enter the holy place, where the priests carried out ceremonial acts of worship. But even the priests weren't allowed to enter the most holy place where God dwelled. Only the high priest could enter the most holy place where God dwelled, and even then only once per year on the Day of Atonement. On this day, when the high priest was to offer a sacrifice for the sins of the people, to come into the presence of God, the priest passed beyond the inner court where the people offered sacrifices, and through the holy place where the priest carried out their everyday responsibilities, beyond the veil and into the holy of holies where God's presence dwelled between the cherubim on the ark of the covenant.

According to God's design, this was a temporary system that served only as a picture of eternal things (Heb. 8:5). Today, God dwells in a temple not made by human hands (Acts 17:24), but in heaven. In order to connect with Him, we need a High Priest who passes not through the sections of an earthly temple, but into the heavenly places. No natural man could be fit for such a task. However, Jesus is no ordinary man, and because He lived the perfect life, He is pure and fit to enter the presence of God.

Without Jesus, we'd never be allowed into God's presence. But because of Jesus, and because God has attributed to all His children the righteousness of Christ, He's given us:

- **The privileges of the priesthood:** It's not only the High Priest who's allowed to go before God—it's all believers. Without Christ's serving as our High Priest, we wouldn't enjoy the freedom to go to God with our worship and prayers. These are among the greatest privileges imaginable.

- **The responsibilities of the priesthood:** Old Testament priests bore the tremendous weight of going before God on behalf of all the people of Israel. Today, we're called not only to use the privilege of connecting with God for our own benefit, but also to intercede for others who aren't connected with God.

If Jesus had never become a man—had He never set aside certain divine privileges and taken on our weakness—He'd never have known what it was like to deal with our struggles. Had He never gone to the cross, He wouldn't know what it was like to suffer beneath the weight of sin. However, Jesus did come. He did die. Therefore, He knows exactly what it's like to endure sin's curse—and He sympathizes deeply with us in our struggles.

Jesus went to great lengths to serve as our great High Priest, and we are called similarly to sympathize with others who suffer under sin's curse. Further, reflecting the priestly ministry of Jesus means we are to move beyond focusing on this present reality, to pass through the heavenly places and into the heavens, and to offer up unceasing prayers on behalf of people God desires to make part of His family.

What is the role of a priest?

Why is it significant that Jesus serves as our great High Priest?

What can you do to serve as a priest for others?

PRAY WITH JESUS

Father, it's such an incredible privilege to come into Your presence. I understand that my sin once separated me from You, but that by the blood of Jesus I'm now allowed to come before You with my prayers and worship. Father, burden my heart for others as I offer up prayers on behalf of my family, friends, and neighbors.

JOURNAL YOUR OWN PRAYER:

"As he approached and saw the city, he wept for it ..." **LUKE 19:41**

Jerusalem is a city of great importance in the life of God's people. The city of David, as it is known, is the capital of Israel, and was home to the temple, the place God's presence dwelt among His people, and the place where Israel worshiped the Lord. Jerusalem, which means "foundation of peace,"[2] is in regard the geographical center of God's work to bring peace to the nations. However, the great city hasn't always lived up to its designation.

When Jesus came to earth, He was born in Bethlehem, but as all Jews were required to regularly visit Jerusalem, He traveled there every year with His parents (Luke 2:41). On one occasion, as His parents were leaving to travel home, Jesus stayed behind without their knowing. When they realized Jesus wasn't with them, they panicked and quickly headed back to the city to look for Him. They finally found Him in the temple discussing the things of God with Israel's teachers.

Jesus, a faithful follower of the law, would travel to Jerusalem for the three required yearly festivals. At Passover, the Jews celebrated God's delivering them from slavery in Egypt. At Pentecost, which was held seven weeks after passover and at the end of the grain harvest, they thanked God for His faithful provision. During the Feast of Booths, the Jews spent a week living in tents as a celebration of God's leading them during their time in the wilderness, and in expressing desire for the eternal kingdom, recognizing our time on earth is temporary. God called His people to return continually to the city of peace to celebrate His goodness to His people—that God made a way for them to avoid the enmity brought by sin and to experience peace in real ways.

However, despite the people's participation in all the festivals and ceremonies, they lost touch with what they represented. As Jesus rode into Jerusalem on that final Sunday before His crucifixion, the people shouted His praises. The crowds "began to praise God joyfully with a loud voice for all the miracles they had seen: Blessed is the King who comes in the name of the Lord. Peace in heaven and glory in the highest heaven!" (Luke 19:37b-38). They'd all heard the news that Jesus had raised Lazarus from the dead—some may have even seen it—and surely someone with this kind of power to perform miracles was the one God had sent to deliver Israel.

However, God's people had seen miracles before. While they were slaves in Egypt, He had sent plagues, including the Passover, which led to their being set free. He'd separated the waters of the Red Sea, then sent it crashing down on their pursuers. He'd healed the waters at Marah, fed them with manna from heaven, caused water to spring forth from a rock, led them through the wilderness by pillars of cloud and fire, and appeared before them in a cloud and thunder and lightning. The Israelites recognized God's power and promised to follow Him. However, they quickly forgot all these things, and devoted themselves to worshiping an image shaped like a calf.

When Jesus rode into Jerusalem, the people acknowledged the power of Jesus and, through their worship, communicated their devotion to the one whom God had sent as King in the line of David. However, Jesus knew about the fickle nature of God's people, and that soon they'd call for His crucifixion. He heard their praises, but He also knew their hearts, and the two didn't line up. Jesus was deeply grieved over the lack of love and devotion the people had for God's Messiah—and He wept.

Today, God isn't enthroned upon a mercy seat in a temple in Jerusalem, but upon the hearts of His people. However, we are surrounded by people whose hearts are utterly devoid of any devotion to God. Many outrightly express their refusal to follow God. However, others profess, like the Jews at Passover, their affections for Jesus, but He knows that their hearts are far from Him.

We need, like Jesus, to mourn this reality—God loves all people and desires they would turn to Him. Our response should be to pray He would intervene, and draw them to Himself.

Why do you think Jesus wept over Jerusalem?

When have you honored God with things you've said, but failed to honor Him in your heart?

Describe feeling burdened for others who profess to follow Jesus but whose lives don't show it. How should you respond to them?

PRAY WITH JESUS

Father, I confess that there are times that I've talked a good talk, but I haven't walked in faithfulness to You. Thank You for Your patience with me! Help me to be truly devoted to You. Further, burden my heart for others who aren't close to You.

JOURNAL YOUR OWN PRAYER:

Session 6
FAITH THAT ENDURES

Focal Passage // Luke 22:31-32

Memory Verse // James 1:12

*Blessed is the one who endures trials, because when
he has stood the test he will receive the crown of life that
God has promised to those who love him.*

Weekly Reading // Luke 16:1-22:34

Most students, during their school years, can't wait to graduate, go to college, then get out into the real world. A lot of people in my city crash into the real world far too soon, and they face challenges many of us could never imagine. Because of some incredibly difficult circumstances, my friend Harold was forced to quit school before graduating. This meant he no longer had to deal with the bullying and fighting (at least not at school), and his schedule was wide open—no more taking the bus through the city at 5:30 a.m., and no more homework (hooray!).

When have you been relieved to finish up something that was difficult?

However, it wasn't all fun and games. Because he was now on his own, Harold had to grow up way too soon and find a way to take care of himself. Along the way, he made some really bad choices, but he also made some good ones. As time passed, having married the love of his life and adding a couple kids to the mix, Harold beat the odds in many ways—he stuck with his wife and took on two full-time jobs to support his family.

At some point, however, Harold recognized that, to have the life he really wanted, he needed to finish his education. So a couple years ago, he enrolled in a program that would allow him to graduate with his high school diploma, and here's what it took. He'd leave the house at 5 a.m. every day to walk (Harold still has no car) to his first job. He'd be off by 3 p.m., walk home to eat an early dinner with his family, then back out the door for his second job on Mondays, Wednesdays, and Fridays, and all day on Saturdays. The other two evenings, Harold was in school for four hours at a time. When he recently graduated, it was one of the most exuberant celebrations I've ever experienced. As Harold puts it, "I was only 19 years late in graduating, but it was worth it!"

We think it takes perseverance to make it through high school—to graduate at 18. Imagine the perseverance required to accomplish what my friend did. It required incredible personal effort, but the truth is that it never would have happened without the support and encouragement of many people.

WATCH

Watch this session's video, and then continue to the group discussion section using the content provided.

SIFTED LIKE WHEAT

We've all heard of situations in which "weeding out" is necessary. Throughout Jesus' ministry, He faced adversity and opposition. He did things in ways no one had seen before, and for many, this was unimaginably good news! For others, however, this new Teacher challenged their way of life, and they were fine with things just the way they were. The Pharisees were Jesus' harshest opposers, and they'd long been looking for ways to destroy Him (Matt. 12:14). But the crowds loved Jesus, and if the Pharisees were to put Him to death, they'd have lost the respect of the people. It was a lose-lose situation. But their hatred was so deep that they continually worked every imaginable angle to plot and plan a scheme that would accomplish their desired end—the death of Jesus.

The disciples, because they were closely associated with Jesus, faced opposition as well. Sure, the Pharisees hated them too, but ultimately, all opposition to God's purposes and God's people comes from Satan. It may seem like we're fighting people, organizations, or systems, but Scripture teaches that our struggle isn't a flesh-and-blood conflict, but one with spiritual forces (Eph. 6:12). Whether we want to be involved or not, we're on the front lines and Satan's soldiers are set against us.

The Passover is perhaps the most important festival celebrated by God's people, because it involves offering the sacrificial lamb for the forgiveness of sins. On this Thursday of what we now call holy week, Jesus and His disciples made preparations for the Passover supper and after sunset as they were together, Jesus washed the feet of His disciples and then enjoyed a meal with them. Knowing that Judas had conspired with the religious leaders to have Jesus killed, Jesus predicted his betrayal. Then, Jesus had some chilling words for Peter—"Satan has asked to sift you like wheat."

Sifting is the process by which wheat kernels—the good part useful for food—is separated from the chaff, or waste. And the procedure is violent. Wheat plants that have been harvested are placed on the ground and beaten with sticks, which breaks the seeds away from the useless parts. All this is then placed in baskets and poured in front of a fan into another basket. The kernels fall and the chaff is blown away. Satan had asked God to sift the disciples. He wanted the opportunity to beat them and drag them through all sorts of difficulties, and to see who would be blown away in the process.

Jesus had faced trials and temptations before beginning His ministry, and they had served to prepare Him for what was to come and to prove His fitness for the task. Jesus knew that trials were useful in helping His followers grow into maturity (James 1:2-4). However, He also knew they were incredibly difficult. Jesus warned Peter, "Look out," a trial is coming your way, and you'd better be ready.

When do you tend to become comfortable or fail to be on guard, and become vulnerable to temptations?

FAITH THAT ENDURES

Jesus warned Peter that he'd face difficulty and temptation. In fact, Jesus predicted Peter's betrayal—for him to "turn back" implies that he would first turn away. Peter was put off by the thought, and practically committed, "For you, Jesus, I'd gladly be thrown into prison. In fact, I'd die for you!"

That Jesus would question his commitment caught Peter totally off guard, and he quickly "corrected" Jesus' thinking—there's no way that will ever happen. But, tragically, Peter was as naïve as he was bold.

We often fall into the same trap. Because we're "good" people—because we've been in church, because we know the Bible, and pray, and even go to camp and on mission trips—we tend to think we've got it together, and that we just won't be tempted by the same kinds of things as other people. However, this is the same kind of thinking that led to Peter's downfall. He loved Jesus, and he knew it, and in a moment of fervor and resolve, Peter truly believed that he'd never turn his back on Jesus. However, life is full of ups and downs, and in our weakest moments, we are certainly vulnerable to the attacks of the devil. And we can be sure that, when we commit ourselves to living for God, the forces of evil will seek to draw us away, destroy us, and defame the name of Jesus.

Peter may not have understood all of this, but Jesus certainly did. There are times we will face struggles and our weaknesses will be exposed, which would warrant much prayer, however, for some reason or another we don't pray. Maybe it's that we don't know how to pray. Perhaps we don't even recognize the need to pray. In those moments, Scripture teaches that the Holy Spirits prays on our behalf. Peter was so confident about his commitment to Jesus, he never even thought to pray that God would protect him from temptation. He certainly never imagined Satan's requesting to sift him like wheat. But Jesus understood these dynamics clearly, and He prayed for Peter.

Since the days of Peter and Jesus, a lot has changed. However, one thing that hasn't changed is that people are people, and we all have weaknesses. Satan will exploit those, so we need to be continually aware of temptations. We'll be tempted to talk badly about others. We'll be tempted to engage in inappropriate relationships with the opposite sex. We'll be tempted to lie, and disobey our parents, and complain, and be selfishly angry. This is why we need to follow Jesus' example:
- To continually ask that God would give us a faith that would not fail
- To pray for friends and loved ones to remain faithful amid temptation

Describe a time you were tempted but endured. What part did prayer play in your victory?

WHEN YOU'VE TURNED BACK

Technically, a blind spot is a defined area where a person's view is obstructed—and we all have them! The problem is that when someone points it out, we're often defensive (after all, we don't see any issues; hint—that's why it's called a blind spot).

- I'm pretty smart, but I made a D on the test—it's because I didn't sleep well last night.
- I'm a good baseball player, but I struck out twice and had a throwing error—it's because my shoulder is sore.

When our friends, coaches, or teachers suggest we make changes, humility says, I think they see something I don't. But pride often keeps us from responding in this way. Nobody likes to have our weaknesses pointed out. We like to think good things about ourselves, and to acknowledge our flaws means admitting maybe I'm not as good as I thought. But sooner or later, as our blind spots come into view, we figure out that we all have many weaknesses.

When Jesus suggested that Peter would turn away, his 'no-way' turned quickly into 'what-have-I-done?!', and his blind spot came blazing into full view. Sure, Jesus had tried to warn Peter about the trial he would face; about an area in his life where, perhaps, he needed to pay special attention. However, Peter wasn't in a place to receive it well, and he missed the opportunity to protect himself and others from a lot of pain.

We, too, are warned to avoid certain choices. But just like Peter, many times we don't listen well, and we pay the price. We'd do well to pay attention to the truths of God's Word, and to avoid living in ways the flesh would tempt us. But the truth is we're all going to make mistakes, even live rebelliously, and sin separates us from Jesus. If we're truly Christians, we will never be eternally separated from God. However, sin does hinder our relationship with Him, and when we do make wrong choices, the answer is always the same—we are to repent. This means literally to turn around. When we find that we've pursued things that offend God, we must turn away from it, and pursue God again.

Just like Jesus predicted, Peter turned his back on Jesus. But Jesus had prayed for him, and once Peter recognized his sin, he did exactly the right thing. He turned away from it, and devoted his life to Jesus all over again. Peter's sin certainly cost him something, but his failings didn't change the purpose God had for him. He followed Jesus' instruction to "strengthen [his] brothers," and Peter was foundational in building the church.

We can take heart in the fact that Jesus, too, prays for us (Rom. 8:34; Heb. 7:25). He desires that we would remain faithful through even the most difficult trials. And He calls us, when we do fail, to turn back—to re-focus ourselves on His purposes, and to serve our brothers and sisters that they, too, would be strengthened.

When have you feared Jesus wouldn't accept you because of your failure? Why is this the wrong way to think?

1. Sifted Like Wheat

All Christians experience testing and trials. God allows these as opportunities to prove our faith, and, further, to help us grow in purity and maturity. If our faith is genuine, we will endure even the most difficult trials by the grace of God.

What is the greatest area of vulnerability in your life?

What practices can you put into place to grow in this area of weakness? How can prayer play an important part?

2. Faith that Endures

When we're in the middle of a trial, many Christians are quick to cry out to God for help. This is certainly a good thing! However, it's not enough. In order to faithfully endure, we need not only to pray in the moment, but in the thousands of moments leading up to a difficult trial.

In what ways are you like Peter—bold, naïve, and a little overconfident—and it keeps you from growing in maturity or depending on God?

How has Satan exploited your weaknesses in the past? How will you make changes in order to endure his attacks don't succeed in the future?

3. When You've Turned Back

When Jesus predicted Peter would turn away, even before any of this actually happened, Jesus said this to Peter—"when you have turned back…" Jesus knew Peter's faith was real, and that he would indeed repent and return to Jesus.

What in your life do you need to repent of in order to return to Christ? Confess your sin or weakness, and tell God of your desire to follow Him.

PRAY LIKE JESUS

Take a few minutes right now to pray for these things. Make it a point to pray:

- That God would help you to be continually aware of temptations, and that He would strengthen you to endure
- That God would use your prayer life to make you strong long before you're faced with trials
- That God would soften your heart so that, when you do sin, you'd be quick to turn from it in pursuing Jesus

DEVO // DAY 1

"In those days Hezekiah became terminally ill. The prophet Isaiah son of Amoz came and said to him, "This is what the LORD says: 'Set your house in order, for you are about to die; you will not recover.'" Then Hezekiah turned his face to the wall and prayed to the LORD, "Please, LORD, remember how I have walked before you faithfully and wholeheartedly and have done what pleases you." And Hezekiah wept bitterly. Isaiah had not yet gone out of the inner courtyard when the word of the LORD came to him: "Go back and tell Hezekiah, the leader of my people, 'This is what the LORD God of your ancestor David says: I have heard your prayer; I have seen your tears. Look, I will heal you. On the third day from now you will go up to the LORD's temple. I will add fifteen years to your life. I will rescue you and this city from the grasp of the king of Assyria. I will defend this city for my sake and for the sake of my servant David.'" **2 KINGS 20:1-6**

At times, we'll be on the proverbial mountaintop and everything in the world seems right. We'd love to build a tent in that spot—and we wouldn't be alone. When Peter witnessed Jesus' transfiguration on top of a literal mountain, he essentially asked, "can't we build shelters here and just hang out for a while?" (Matt. 17:4). But this isn't the way it works. These days certainly enrich our faith, but we can't expect everything to be extraordinarily sweet all the time. Most days are pretty ordinary. We get up, go about our business, eat our green beans, then get back to it the following day. These days are important to our faith as well. During these seasons, we learn to practice discipline, and we grow in our understanding of what it means to follow God as a matter of devotion, not emotion.

At other times, our faith will be utterly tested. We'll experience circumstances that bring us to say in desperation, *there's no way I will ever make it through this! God help me!*

Hezekiah ruled over Judah for 29 years beginning at the age of 25. He was one of the few kings devoted to God, and the Bible says of Hezekiah that he was more zealous for God than any of the previous kings (2 Kings 18:5). Because God put Hezekiah first in his personal life as well as in all the things he pursued as Judah's leader, the Lord prospered him.

However, the prosperity God provided was threatened by the Assyrians, the most powerful nation in the world at the time. They'd already conquered the northern kingdom, and now they were marching against Jerusalem, openly defying the God of Judah, calling Him powerless like the gods of all the nations they'd conquered. Hezekiah knew nothing better to do than cry out to God, so he prayed—"Now, LORD our God, please save us from his power so that all the kingdoms of the earth may know that you, LORD, are God—you alone" (2 Kings 19:19). His prayer didn't focus on his own personal comfort, or the safety of the people, but on the glory of God. This is a picture of this king's heart.

God answered Hezekiah's prayer and supernaturally defended His people. Soon after, however, Hezekiah became critically ill. In fact, things were looking so bad that Isaiah came to him with this message.

Hezekiah's faith had been tested plenty of times before, and he'd seen God's faithfulness on display in powerful ways. But this was different. He not only faced a difficult situation—Hezekiah had a message from God Himself stating that his time was up. The devastating news may have made Hezekiah want to crawl in bed, hide away, and just give up. However, that wasn't his style. He did what he'd no doubt done many times before when he faced difficult circumstances—he prayed.

Despite facing circumstances that put him to the test and stretched his faith to the limits, Hezekiah trusted God and demonstrated that trust through a life of obedience and prayer. God answered with healing. At times, our circumstances will seem impossible to overcome. However, Jesus has prayed for us. Further, we ourselves have the privilege of sharing our hearts with God. When we feel overwhelmed, God invites us to be honest. He desires deeply that we would endure, and when we ask for His help, He'll no doubt offer it.

When have circumstances been overwhelming to the point you questioned God's goodness?

How has God proven faithful to you in difficult times?

How will you demonstrate faith like Hezekiah in your prayer life?

PRAY WITH JESUS

Father, there have been sweet times when all in my world has been right—thank You for those. There are also times when life is difficult and I wonder if I'm going to make it through. Thank You for helping me during those times. Help me to depend on You at all times.

JOURNAL YOUR OWN PRAYER:

DEVO // DAY 2

"Because he has his heart set on me, I will deliver him; I will protect him because he knows my name. When he calls out to me, I will answer him; I will be with him in trouble. I will rescue him and give him honor. I will satisfy him with a long life and show him my salvation."
PSALM 91:14-16

From the time of his rebellion, Satan had set himself against God and His purposes, and is intent on destroying God's people. In the creation account, God blessed Adam and Eve with many freedoms, and one condition—don't eat from the tree in the middle of the garden. If they did, God warned that they would die. Satan knew of the consequences of their disobedience, which is exactly why he deceived them, tempting them to go against God's commands. He wanted them to die. In the New Testament, we read that the devil is like a roaring like, roaming the earth and looking for people to devour (1 Pet. 5:8).

If this was all there is to the story, it would be quite a frightening reality. However there's more—and it's great news! Though Satan and his forces are formidable enemies, through His death and resurrection, Jesus crushed Satan's power, fulfilling God's promise to the devil in Genesis 3:15. By the cross, "the ruler of this world has been judged" and is condemned for eternity. One day Jesus will completely destroy Satan's power, however, as it stands now, the devil is allowed a level of authority in the world, and does everything in his power to lead people astray. This is why it's so important that we depend continually on God for protection.

In Psalm 91, the author mentions a myriad of terrors, which are left undefined so that we can apply the principles to any fear we may face. Today, we may not suffer the dangers that are listed, but if we're honest with ourselves, there are fears we certainly all face. A few things teenagers are commonly afraid of are:

- **Tests and poor academic performance:** Not passing often makes students think, I'm a failure.
- **Talking with parents about personal issues:** *If they know what I've done, they'll never forgive me.*
- **Not fitting in at school:** The people we're surrounded by go a long way in determining our experience.
- **Life after graduation:** Success in our culture is measured according to an unrealistic social media standard, and teens often feel they can never measure up.
- **Home life:** Tough things happen in the home that are simply out of a teen's control.[1]

We may not experience arrows flying by our faces, plagues and pestilence, or dangers from wild animals (there are Christians in the world who certainly do), but in America today we do experience real difficulties that create legitimate fear and insecurity. When we experience fear, the appropriate response is to turn to God. For those who live "under the protection of the Most High," no harm will come to us.

This doesn't mean we will never suffer harm in this life. Look at the life of Jesus—He's the only man in history to live the perfect life, and He suffered the worst death imaginable. But Jesus challenged us to see things from a heavenly perspective. "Don't fear those who kill the body but are not able to kill the soul; rather, fear him who is able to destroy both soul and body in hell" (Matt. 10:28). In this life, our bodies are vulnerable to all kinds of dangers, from diseases to car crashes to people bent on doing evil. We will one day (unless Jesus returns first) experience the fullest expression of sin's violence on our bodies—death. However, even then, we have no need to fear in the ultimate sense, because God has promised to take care of His children in the ultimate sense.

When we cry out to Him in prayer, God hears. When our hearts are set on Him, He answers. Because God loves us, He rescues us from trouble and rewards us with eternal life.

What is something that has caused you real fear?

How has God comforted you when you've experienced times of fear? How might God use you to comfort others?

Considering God answers when we call to Him in trouble, how can you incorporate prayer into your everyday life to help deal with fear?

PRAY WITH JESUS

Father, I deal with difficult things that sometimes cause me to fear. I know that You love me and that You've promised to take care of me. Help me to trust in You.

JOURNAL YOUR OWN PRAYER:

DEVO // DAY 3

"Pray to the Lord for me," Simon replied, "so that nothing you have said may happen to me." **ACTS 8:24**

One of the greatest privileges of being part of God's family is belonging to a church. Together, we get to do incredibly important things, such as study God's Word and worship. Beyond these, we enjoy a lot of non-essentials too. At our church, we have cookouts and watch movies together, kids play soccer every week, we serve the community together, and get together for football games. There are all kinds of great things that happen in a church.

However, it's not all fun and games. Chances are that, in any given church, there are people facing the most difficult challenges imaginable. It's not uncommon, when we learn of these things, to ask, *what can I do for you?* We've all asked this question, right? The only response that is perhaps more common is, *I'll pray for you.*

At times, we say this without necessarily considering the weight behind it, as if praying is no big deal. However, in all reality, one of the best things (if not the best thing) we can do for someone who's struggling, is to pray. We're called to pray for one another (Eph. 6:18), and prayer truly makes a difference in the lives of those for whom we intercede.

In Acts 8, we find Philip, having fled Jerusalem because of Saul's persecution against the church, preaching the gospel for the first time in Samaria. Further, by the power of Christ, he healed many who were sick and delivered many from demonic oppression. The crowds were amazed, listened to the message Philip preached, and many came to faith.

Among the crowds was a man named Simon who was known for signs and wonders as well. He had amazed the Samaritans through practicing sorcery. However, the people were now turning to Jesus, and even Simon believed. He began following Philip as he traveled, ministering to people in the name of Jesus. When Simon witnessed the apostles laying hands on the Samaritan people, and that they received the Spirit, Simon also wanted this ability. So he offered money to the apostles. Peter's response shocked Simon: "May your silver be destroyed with you, because you thought you could obtain the gift of God with money!" (Acts 8:20b).

Simon had previously "believed" the gospel, but now, Peter declared that he'd suffer destruction. We see, in response to Peter's warning, a measure of repentance in Simon: "'Pray to the Lord for me,' Simon replied, 'so that nothing you have said may happen to me'" (Acts 8:24).

Satan had asked of the Lord to sift Peter like wheat—to beat him until he broke loose of his faith, then to shake him inside a sifting screen until he fell through the holes, separated from the faith that bound him to Christ. Satan wanted similarly to attack Simon's faith. Here's the thing. Genuine faith transforms us, becomes an essential part of who we are, and can never be separated from us.

Did Simon have genuine faith, or a counterfeit, intellectual kind of belief? The Bible doesn't give us enough details that we can know how the story ends. However, history does tell many details of his story.[2] After the episode we see in Acts, he traveled to Caesarea and continued to deceive. Peter went there to confront him publicly about the false doctrines he claimed. Legend has it that Simon offered to prove his divinity by flying—he trusted the demons that allowed him to perform signs would make this happen. But Peter prayed that the Lord wouldn't allow this, and Simon fell to the ground. He was badly injured, but survived, and he took his own life.

There was a difference between the sifting of Peter's versus Simon's faith. Whereas Peter, after betraying the Lord, was genuinely broken-hearted over his sin, Simon wanted to be spared the consequences of his sin, but expressed no repentance about dishonoring the Lord.

How do we know for sure if someone's faith is real? Quite simply—we can't. However, we can know that, just as he did with Peter and Simon, Satan demands the opportunity to sift every person who would come to faith in Christ. So the next time you tell someone, I'll pray for you—do it! The trial they're facing may be a test of their faith, and our prayers are powerful in helping them walk in humility and victory.

Describe a time you were criticized by other believers for dishonoring God.

How has your faith been tested? What helped you to "pass" the test?

How would God have you pray for yourself concerning current trials? In preparation for future trials? For others?

PRAY WITH JESUS

Father, there are times when I'm concerned more with the consequences of my sins than I am with the fact that my sin dishonors You. Help me to be, above all, devoted to your glory. Thank You for helping me hold onto my faith during difficult times.

JOURNAL YOUR OWN PRAYER:

DEVO // DAY 4

"Who is to condemn? Christ Jesus is the one who died—more than that, who was raised—who is at the right hand of God, who indeed is interceding for us." **ROMANS 8:34**

Throughout the middle school and high school years, teenagers are sure to hear a wide range of mixed messages about themselves:

- **Parents:** We believe in you, you can do anything!
- **Grandparents:** Aren't you just the most precious little thing in the world.
- **Friends:** It's great to hang out!
- **Mean girls:** You look so icky…
- **Teachers:** You have to start thinking about college.
- **Coaches:** Get your rear end into gear!
- **Marketing:** You can never be happy without this latest, coolest item.
- **The media:** You'll never measure up to the perfect standard of these movie stars.

We receive these messages, and infinitely more. And for some of us, one or more of these may land a little closer to home than others. We're continually subject to a barrage of messages about ourselves, and if we're not careful, we'll begin to define ourselves according to the messages that resonate most in a given moment.

Tragically, teenagers in America today suffer from anxiety and depression more than at any other time in history,[3] and this is due, in a certain sense, to their buying into unhealthy messages. Culture says, when your grades aren't good enough, you're a failure! If you're not as good looking as all the other teens on social media, you're worthless! For some reason, among all the messages we receive from many sources, the negative ones tend to ring out a little more clearly in our minds. And if we don't have the skills or ammunition to fight them off, they can cause real pain and damage.

Condemnation, on a certain level, means to express wholehearted disapproval. Tragically, many of us face disapproval because the standards to which we're held simply aren't healthy. When a teen girl lives modestly and conservatively, she's often left out or cut off. She often experiences pressures to conform to worldly patterns. After all, everyone's doing it! When a guy chooses to treat others respectfully, refusing to engage in inappropriate behaviors that so many others do, he's often made fun of—what's wrong with you? It's pretty simple. When we do what's right, culture disapproves. Condemns.

However, in the fullest sense, to condemn is to hand down a severe sentence—particularly, death. There may be times, due to the unkindness of others, that we'd wish God would go ahead and take us. However, though many may act like it's their place, no person on earth has the right to determine anyone else's worth. No one has the right to condemn us.

When God made people, He created us in His image and with a specific purpose. Our worth flows directly from that, and isn't subject to the perspectives and opinions of the culture, of our peers, or anyone else. Only God has the right to bless or condemn, and if we choose moment by moment to live in obedience to Christ, God approves of us, and what others think simply doesn't matter.

However, it doesn't always feel like that, right? When others say hurtful things or we're lonely because our friends are out doing things we refuse to participate in, it feels like it matters a lot! Peter felt this too. He knew following Christ was ultimately right, but his heart told him (wrongly!) associating with Jesus would get him into big trouble, and it wasn't worth it. He was afraid, so he turned away. But Jesus prayed that Peter would return, and He's continually praying for us as well.

How have you, in real ways, experienced the condemnation of the world?

How do you typically respond in order to show the difference Jesus makes in your life? How can you respond better in the future?

How does Jesus' praying for you give you encouragement to ignore the world's condemnation and focus on His approval?

PRAY WITH JESUS

Father, when I experience disapproval for doing the right things, it definitely hurts. When this happens, help me to respond with kindness in order to show the love of Christ. Also, help me to seek Your approval above all others.

JOURNAL YOUR OWN PRAYER:

"Be on your guard, so that your minds are not dulled from carousing, drunkenness, and worries of life, or that day will come on you unexpectedly like a trap. For it will come on all who live on the face of the whole earth. But be alert at all times, praying that you may have strength to escape all these things that are going to take place and to stand before the Son of Man." **LUKE 21:34-36**

It's been said that more people need to put down the magnifying glass and pick up a mirror. Most people tend to look critically at others' lives, noticing the finer points of their misbehaving, and full of good insights as to how they could improve. All the while, we have trouble identifying our own weaknesses. This is a matter of awareness, and we're often highly aware of others (particularly their mistakes) and have little honest awareness of ourselves.

Have you ever been in a restaurant, and someone at a table nearby is laughing so loudly the entire restaurant could hear. Maybe it was someone at your table—and you weren't only embarrassed, but embarrassed for them. If you've never experienced this, it was probably you, and might not have even been aware!

Healthy self-awareness begins with understanding that we all have our fair share of weaknesses and plenty of room for growth. We may be tempted at times to think we have it all together. However, if we'll stop focusing on others, and instead pick up a mirror, we'll find all kinds of imperfections.

In Luke 21, Jesus told us to be on guard—to be aware of our surroundings, and aware of our tendencies to engage and respond in unhealthy ways. Some of us may be tempted to engage in partying. After all, we think, what's wrong with sowing a few wild oats? Everybody does it, and one day after I've had my fun, I'll straighten out. Jesus says this deadens our minds and keeps us from focusing on eternal things. Be aware, engaging in these things comes with great risk!

Others, though they refuse to participate in behaviors that are "really bad," get caught up in a lifestyle that doesn't seem terribly wrong on the surface, but which draws them to misplace affections owed to Jesus. When we throw ourselves fully into academics or sports, into video games or relationships, and we don't have time or attention for Jesus, these "worries of life" keep us from honoring God. Jesus says, we need to look out for these sorts of tendencies in our lives.

One day very soon, Jesus will return and we will be judged based on the ways we've lived. If we've lived by faith and in submission to Christ, we will be rewarded. But if we've been caught up in the ways of the world, no matter what we think about ourselves, we'll be condemned. Jesus warns that, for those who are unaware, that day will catch them off guard, and it will be too late. However, today we have the opportunity to put ourselves in a great position to face the judgment. We're called to be aware of the things happening in the world, and perhaps more importantly, of our own hearts. When we humbly admit our weaknesses, and pray that God would strengthen us to stand the day of judgment, God will provide the awareness and strength we need to live well.

When has God helped you to see a weakness in your life you were unaware of?

What do you struggle with that causes you to worry about facing judgment? What safeguards will you put in place to help deal with this weakness?

How will you commit to praying so that you grow in awareness?

PRAY WITH JESUS

Father, there are times I get caught up in the cares of the world, and I lose focus on eternal things. Help me to be aware of my tendencies, help me to own up to my weaknesses, and strengthen me in those areas so I can live for You.

JOURNAL YOUR OWN PRAYER:

Session 7
FOR THE FATHER'S WILL

Focal Passage // Luke 22:39-46

Memory Verse // 1 John 5:14-15

This is the confidence we have before him: If we ask anything according to his will, he hears us. And if we know that he hears whatever we ask, we know that we have what we have asked of him.

Weekly Reading // Luke 22:35-22:71

Teenagers in general want to please their parents. We understand that our parents are older and wiser, and that they're responsible to help us make healthy choices. Beyond this, we want to *honor* our parents. God has given them a position of authority in our lives, and it's our duty to show respect. On top of these, our parents provide all sorts of things for us—pizza and new shoes, a comfy bed, vacations and video games, even a new cell phone when we need it. Our parents are always there for us, and even if our parents aren't perfect (every parent is far from perfect), they love us no matter what.

Because of this, we'll do the best we can to obey. I remember when I was in high school, I fell in love with music and every Sunday night, after church then dinner with friends, we'd go back to the church to sing. Sounds like every parent's dream, right? Yes, except that my curfew was 10 p.m. on Sunday evenings, and without fail I'd end up rushing out with only five minutes to get home. The problem was, I lived ten minutes away.

Describe a time when you failed to follow through in obeying your parents. What were the consequences?

Because my parents were good to me, and, honestly, because of their position in my life, I genuinely desired to do what they asked, *except* when it interfered with what I wanted. This is the problem with the way many people see authority in their lives. We look at obeying rules in terms of a threshold. If the cost is low and the benefit is great, we're happy to obey. But when it's the other way around and the decision meets a certain cost-benefit threshold—when we think it's "worth" it—we disobey. After all, *staying out all night was worth the punishment I'd receive.*

This sort of "obedience" may appear to be a demonstration of respect for our parents. However, it's certainly not honor. In Scripture we're called to obey as a matter of the heart. As Jesus grew nearer and nearer to the cross, the cost living in obedience would require was extremely difficult to bear. However, He never wavered. His Father was worthy of honor. His Father had related to Him in all the ways a Father should. As a sign of humility and honor, Jesus chose obedience—not because of the "threshold," but because He truly valued the will of the Father even over His own desires.

Watch this session's video, and then continue to the group discussion section using the content provided.

THAT YOU MAY NOT FALL INTO TEMPTATION

A big event in every high schooler's life, at least for those planning to go to college, is taking the ACT or SAT exams. I took my ACT exam in December of my junior year, and I remember being nervous beyond words the night before. After all, my whole future rested on how I performed (okay, maybe I'm being a little melodramatic). But test anxiety—a deep sense of worry or fear of failing, and accompanied by physical symptoms such as tension or nausea—is a real thing, and it's something that over one third of students experience.[1]

Here's the thing about tests—they're not supposed to be easy. They're meant to push our limits; to determine the thresholds of our abilities, our knowledge, or our commitment. If I wanted to test my strength, I could throw 475 pounds on a bar and try to bench press it, but it would literally kill me! If I put 65 pounds on, it would be easy, but it wouldn't be a test. To test my strength, we'd have to find exactly the right weight that would push me to my limit—that's right on the line—but that I could successfully carry out.

The disciples had been tested many times throughout their time with Jesus. He'd called them to leave everything to follow Him—and they did. He'd sent them out to minister to the surrounding villages—and they went. He'd authorized them to heal and preach, and they did these things with confidence and authority. But soon, they'd face a test unlike anything they could imagine.

"As usual," Jesus made His way to the Mount of Olives. He encouraged the disciples to pray that they would be ready for the tests they'd soon face. Jesus had even prayed for them, that their faith would not fail beneath the weight they'd soon bear. This time, though, He prayed for Himself.

Jesus was seriously tested in the wilderness before beginning His public ministry—and He passed with flying colors—but the trial coming up in a matter of hours would push Him to the limit. We get stressed about having to solve a few math problems; imagine facing the cross! But Jesus was prepared. He'd done all the right things throughout His life, including continually praying in order to stay connected with the Father and to remain empowered by the Spirit. And in the moments before He'd face this ultimate test, He did what He'd done many times before—Jesus went to one of His favorite spots to pray.

What sort of pressures are you facing in your life? How would prayer make a difference in helping you deal with those?

NOT MY WILL BUT YOURS

While the disciples were praying (at least they were supposed to be), Jesus stepped away in order to get alone with the Father. He was close with His disciples, but His connection with the Father was unique—the Father and Son are literally united as one, not physically, but in essence relationally and spiritually (John 17:21). And as He was overwhelmed with dread over the suffering He'd soon face, Jesus wanted to be with His Father.

As He knelt down to pray, Jesus was only "a stone's throw" away from the disciples, at least in a physical sense. But in a spiritual sense, He was miles away. The disciples were sleeping, but Jesus was praying. They were overwhelmed by physical and fleshly weakness, but Jesus was, even aside from being physically exhausted, as acutely spiritually focused as ever.

Jesus had come to earth to deal with the problem of sin in the world, and He knew that from eternity past God had ordained His death as the means of redemption (1 Pet. 1:18-21). In His omniscience, He knew He would die, and He had predicted His death multiple times. However, on this night, the full reality of His imminent suffering came to bear upon His humanity—and this was something He simply did not want to experience! So He begged God, "Father, if you are willing, take this cup away from me" (Luke 22:42).

Just the night before, Jesus had taken the Passover meal with His disciples. He shared the cup with them, which represented His sacrifice—His blood. The cup served as a reminder of God's promise to send the Messiah who would redeem fallen humanity. For generations, God's people had waited for the fulfillment of that promise, yet they didn't understand the rescue did not require political prowess and military might, but sacrifice for the payment of sin. Jesus shared the cup with His disciples as a symbol of what He'd soon experience. Now it was time He drank the cup alone.

Despite that He desired to be freed from the burden of the cross, because Jesus was fully surrendered to the Father's will, He willingly submitted. In response to Jesus' prayer, an angel visited Him, supplying Him with supernatural strength for the trials ahead. Because Jesus was fully human, and in order to experience our reality, He had to set aside certain divine abilities, He needed help from above to live in complete obedience.

Though the cup wouldn't be removed from Jesus, God would provide supernatural strength so that Jesus would faithfully endure the trials of His passion.

When has God called you to do something you weren't necessarily excited about? How did you respond?

DROPS OF BLOOD

I was raised in a family in which my parents were really good to me. They often took me and my friends to the movies. They bought me the shoes I wanted, and they provided a pretty nice car for me to drive. I even got an allowance every week that I could spend pretty much any way I pleased. However, these things didn't come without a measure of responsibility. If I wanted the benefits, I had to pay the price, and this involved, among other things, taking care of our yard. No big deal, right? Except that our "lawn" was a ten acre farm! Every week, the trimming alone took me almost three hours, and there were times I was so hot and tired I felt like I might die (which I clearly expressed to my parents from time to time, but they didn't care). Describe a time you said something to the effect of, *I feel like I'm going to die.*

When we exert ourselves, we sometimes joke about dying, but the truth is death is no joking matter. When Adam and Eve chose sin over faithful obedience to God, the sentence God handed down was death—physically and spiritually. Because every human has sinned, every one of us has experienced death in real ways, and we will one day experience physical death in the fullest sense (apart from Christ's returning in our lifetime). However, because God loves us, He was not content to let us remain unhindered on our path toward death. The answer all along, was *Jesus*!

As Jesus grew ever closer to His death on the cross, He felt the pressure of the moment, and asked God to find another way to deal with the consequences of sin. The Father's answer was a resounding *no*, and as if Jesus hadn't already dealt with enough, the pressure He felt became increasingly heavy. In fact, the anguish He experienced was so severe that Jesus not only felt as if He might die, He was actually near death (Matt. 26:38). As we would expect, Jesus' response was to continue in prayer, and as He did His sweat turned to blood. Bloody sweat is a very rare medical condition that causes blood to ooze from the skin, usually around the face, when the blood vessels below the skin break open. This is usually caused by extreme distress or fear, such as facing death, torture, or severe ongoing abuse.[2]

In the moments leading up to the cross, Jesus was fighting the most intense spiritual battle of His life. He'd called on His closest followers to pray, but they were sleeping. He'd faced the devil alone in the desert, and that experience had helped prepare Him for this very moment. Prior to the former temptation, Jesus had prayed and the Holy Spirit came upon Him to strengthen Him for the impending battle. This time, regardless of being exhausted and despite the dread and fear, even with blood pouring out of the pores in His face, Jesus pressed forward in prayer and obedience. And just like before, the Father looked upon His Son with pleasure, and sent a ministering spirit to strengthen Him.

When have you desperately needed God to supply you with strength? How did you rely on prayer in this time?

1. That You May Not Fall into Temptation

Jesus knew that He and the disciples would soon face very strong temptations. Jesus would be betrayed, put on trial, and crucified, and He didn't want to endure these things. Remaining faithful would require God's strength, so Jesus devoted Himself to prayer.

How did Jesus' patterns—His "usual" rhythms—help Him remain steadfast in pursuing God's purposes for His life?

How does prayer help us to walk successfully through difficult situations?

2. Not My Will But Yours

Jesus was devoted to the Father's will even above His own desires. That we would experience God's blessings required Jesus' dying on the cross, and to follow Christ requires that we take up our cross daily. This means we must be continually willing to put to death our own desires that are contrary to God's, devoting ourselves instead to His purposes.

Describe a time you intentionally set aside your own desires to follow Christ. How did that affect your faith?

What part does prayer play in killing sin in our lives that we may live for Jesus?

3. Drops of Blood

Even under stress, Jesus never acted selfishly or sinfully. Because He was, above all other things, committed to honoring God, He surrendered to the Father's will.

When has someone paid a great price in order that you could receive something good?

When has doing the right thing cost you greatly? How can your prayer life help you to grow in living sacrificially?

PRAY LIKE JESUS

Take a few minutes right now to pray for these things. Make it a point to pray:

- That God would help you to pray every day in ways that would make you strong to endure temptations
- That God would conform your desires to His
- That, when you feel intense pressure, you wouldn't fall back into sinful patterns, but that the fruit of the Spirit would be born out in your life

*"This is what your Lord says—the L*ORD*, even your God, who defends his people—'Look, I have removed from your hand the cup that causes staggering; that goblet, the cup of my fury. You will never drink it again.'"* **ISAIAH 51:22**

When I was in school, baseball was a sport I took pretty seriously, and by the time I was in seventh grade, I'd been playing for about seven years, and I'd developed pretty solid fundamentals. However, one day while we were taking fielding practice, I bent down to field a ground ball and it popped up and hit me right in the mouth! Not a glancing blow, but a square in the teeth, blood everywhere, writhing in pain kind of blow. I'd learned over the years I'm supposed to, as I'd heard my coach yell a million times, stay down on the ball! However, on that particular summer afternoon, I learned another lesson—sometimes staying down means being hit in the face by a hard object. Moving forward, I knew in my mind to keep my glove down, but my fear kept me from following through, and I made several errors as I worked through that.

Life consists of learning lessons and making healthy choices. When God entered into a relationship with Israel, He taught them many lessons about healthy living. He revealed to them that being honest, choosing kindness, avoiding violence, and above all, honoring Him, would bring blessings in their lives. However, to live contrary to these would bring all sorts of unwanted consequences.

Tragically, Israel failed to follow through consistently on the things God had called them to, and they experienced the correction He'd warned them about—and the consequences were severe! Their homeland was conquered by foreign powers, they were taken as captives to another country, and they were cut off from the blessings of God. Scripture often uses a cup as a metaphor for God's wrath, and God's people had drunk so much of God's wrath they couldn't think straight (Isa. 51:21).

Sometimes, we engage in behaviors we know aren't good for us, but in the moment it feels good or it's fun, so we do it anyway. Perhaps, in the past we've done similar things. We felt guilty—maybe even paid a steep price—and we "learned our lesson." Yet, we still do the same things again and again. When we do this we're giving up control to fleshly desires. If we were wise, we would confess our wrongdoing and repent. But the problem is that far too many of us keep going, continuing to pour into our lives the things we know aren't good for us.

God's people had sinned continually, and they'd drunk a good portion of God's wrath when He came to them with a promise. God defends His people—He pleads on their behalf— and He revealed that He would remove the cup. He'd cease pouring out His fury on their disobedience, He'd cause them to return to Him, and, best of all, they'd never have to drink from the cup again!

Today, we have an accuser, Satan, who continually points out to God all the things we do wrong. *Look at this one—his heart is full of lust. Punish him! Look at her—she gossips nonstop. She deserves your worst!* And the truth is that we are all guilty of sin, and we do deserve God's punishment.

When Jesus was praying in the garden, He asked God to remove the cup of His wrath. However, this wasn't God's plan, and Jesus, who never committed a single sin, drank the cup.

On the other hand, when we turn away from pursuing the things of the world, though we have sinned, God removes the curse and gives us blessing, and, because of Jesus, we "will never drink [the cup] again." Though the devil will continue to accuse, we can know that Christ intercedes for us, God defends us, and we will be spared God's fury for eternity.

When have you been accused of wrongdoing? How did you respond?

Why must God punish sin? Why do you deserve to be spared from His wrath?

How should God's defending you impact the ways you live? The ways you pray?

PRAY WITH JESUS

Father, I know that, because I've sinned, I deserve Your wrath. Thank You for Jesus' sacrifice, and that, in my place, He drank the cup. Help me to live in continual repentance as an expression of my devotion and gratitude.

JOURNAL YOUR OWN PRAYER:

"I sought the LORD, and he answered me and rescued me from all my fears. Those who look to him are radiant with joy; their faces will never be ashamed. This poor man cried, and the LORD heard him and saved him from all his troubles." **PSALM 34:4-6**

In Scripture, we hear God calling to His people hundreds of times, "Don't be afraid."

When God appeared to Abram in a vision, He told him there was no reason to be afraid (Gen. 15:1). He told Moses there was no reason to fear foreign armies (Num. 21:34). When Joshua was fighting for the promised land, God told him not to be afraid of the powerful people who dwelled there (Jos. 10:8). When an angel appeared to Gideon, he was terrified, but God told him there was no reason to fear (Judges 6:23). When Jesus came to the disciples walking on the water, they thought He was a ghost and they were terribly afraid. Jesus called out to them, "Don't be afraid" (Matt. 14:27).

We read of similar instances over and over again. In David's life, there were many times he had a legitimate reason to be afraid. While he was watching sheep, there were multiple times he needed to defend them against wild animals, including a lion and a bear. When Goliath scorned God's people, David went out against him. When he was a young man, King Saul tried over and over again to take David's life. And later on, David's own son, Absalom, sought his father's life in seeking the throne for himself.

After David became king over Israel, God came to him with a specific promise. God told David that, through his rule, God would provide a secure home for Israel, that He would give rest from enemies, and that He would establish David's house forever. Because of God's promise to bless and preserve him, and because David had seen God's hand in his life many times before, he had a deep trust in God to deliver him through even the most difficult and terrifying trials.

In Psalm 34, David revisits the times when he was afraid. Whereas, when we encounter frightening situations, our reaction may be to run away, to fight back, or just shut down, David's natural response was to seek the Lord. God's response was to rescue David from his fears.

When Jesus faced a difficult situation, He essentially called out to God, "please deliver me from this suffering. Take this cup from me." But God's response to Jesus was different than to David. He didn't deliver Jesus from the suffering He so desperately wanted to avoid.

If God had delivered Jesus, then we would have a million reasons to be afraid, for we would be left to deal with our sins on our own. However, through Jesus' death on the cross, He's paid for the sins of God's people, and we have no reason to fear.

When David was afraid, he cried out to God in prayer. In Christ, we have the same promises—even better promises—as David. We are called to come to God with our cares, knowing that He hears, and that He will rescue us from our troubles.

What causes you to be afraid?

How has God demonstrated that He will take care of you?

How has prayer played a part in helping you work through your fears? How can you pray with even more dedication in the future?

PRAY WITH JESUS

Father, there are times when I feel insecure and afraid because there are a lot of things that I simply can't control. Help me to trust that You are in control, and to know that You will take care of me.

JOURNAL YOUR OWN PRAYER:

"About midnight Paul and Silas were praying and singing hymns to God, and the prisoners were listening to them." **ACTS 16:25**

Paul and Silas were missionaries committed to taking the gospel to people who didn't know Jesus. As they traveled sharing the good news, they were continually met with all kinds of resistance. During one instance, they were confronted by a girl who was possessed by an evil spirit, and she continually harassed the missionaries as they sought to reach people with the good news.

Paul felt the same way we likely would have—he was irritated! But not with the girl. Being extremely annoyed with the spirit, by the authority that Christ had given the apostles, Paul did one of the kindest things imaginable for the girl—he commanded the spirit to set her free. The spirit had no choice but to leave. This was a great thing for the girl, however, it was also complicated. She worked for masters who had made money from her ability to predict the future, and with the demon's being gone, she no longer had this ability. When the owners realized their way of making money was gone, they brought false charges against Paul and Silas, and had them beaten and thrown in jail.

As Christians, we know we're supposed to be kind to others. Further, we know we're to live this way simply because it's the right thing to do, and with no concern for how people respond. However, if we're honest, when we're intentionally kind and others don't respond the ways we think they should, we're often annoyed in wrong ways.

Paul and Silas had done all the right things—they'd left their home to take the gospel to lost people, and they'd set a young girl free from demonic oppression—but they were met with the worst response imaginable. The beating they received was with rods tied together in a bundle, a severe form of punishment. Further, this treatment was illegal since they hadn't been convicted of any crime. Further, they weren't treated like your average criminal. They were placed in the most secure part of the prison with the most violent offenders, and placed in stocks, a device which locked prisoners' legs into place, and which was very painful. We may be tempted to think that, at this point, they were overwhelmed by the what they'd experienced, finally realized their situation was hopeless, and gave in to worry and depression.

However, just the opposite is true. Just as Jesus, when He faced the pressures and troubles of serving others, made it a point to engage more earnestly in prayer, in Acts 16, we don't find Paul and Silas wallowing in their misery. Instead, amid the worst circumstances, they were worshiping and praying.

It's easy to live well when life is going great. Even non-believers do this. However, when we face intense pressure and pain, it's then we have a great opportunity to demonstrate the difference God makes in our lives. But we can't do it on our own. Many have tried, by their own power, to grin and bear it, only to have failed miserably. In order to reflect the goodness of God in the middle of difficult times, we must depend on the power of God. This is why prayer is so important. By our prayers, we communicate to God that we can't do it on our own, and we need Him to provide us with the power to live well through hardship.

God's response to Paul and Silas was a miracle—He sent an earthquake that shook free their shackles and set all the prisoners free. And because of Paul and Silas' choices, the jailer and all his family came to faith in Jesus. When we live faithfully and prayerfully through troubles, God will use us to impact others as well.

Describe a time when you've shown kindness to someone and they responded in a way you didn't appreciate.

When have you seen God use difficulties in your life to provide an opportunity to reveal the goodness of Him to others?

What prayer habits do you need to establish to prepare yourself to respond well to trouble?

PRAY WITH JESUS

Father, to be honest, I naturally want to do everything I can to avoid trouble; however, I understand that sometimes You use difficult circumstances in my life for Your glory. Please help me to live in full dependence on You so that when I do face hardships, people will see Your power in my life.

JOURNAL YOUR OWN PRAYER:

"During his earthly life, he offered prayers and appeals with loud cries and tears to the one who was able to save him from death, and he was heard because of his reverence." **HEBREWS 5:7**

A common question to ask someone in getting to know them is, "If you could meet anyone in the world, living or dead, who would it be?" If you answered, "Jesus," well, you're not really playing by the rules, but it definitely says something about you. If you answered Abraham Lincoln, Shakespeare, or Elvis, though it may reveal the things you appreciate, there's no way you'll ever actually meet them. If, on the other hand, you wanted to meet the president or today's most popular movie stars or musicians, your chances are slightly better in those scenarios than meeting people who have died. However, you're not going to simply strut into the living room of any the world's most famous or most powerful people. If you wanted to gain an audience, you'd have to go through someone authorized to introduce you.

In the Old Testament, God's people could only approach Him through a high priest. They couldn't come into His presence any time they desired, and even the priests had to meet certain requirements, including participating in elaborate ceremonial rituals to prepare for entering God's presence. We still live according to this reality—we absolutely cannot approach God except through a high priest. Except today it looks different. No longer do we come before God through an earthly priest, but through Jesus, our eternal High Priest.

As Jesus approached the cross, He felt an immense weight. Soon, He'd literally bear the weight of the world's sin. On the evening leading up to His betrayal, He went to the garden to take advantage of His priestly privileges. He'd make one final appeal to God, crying out in anguish, Lord, please spare me from this death.

On one level, He wanted to be spared from the suffering involved in bearing the Lord's wrath. However, in the fullest sense, He was asking God to rescue Him from remaining in death.

The Father heard Jesus' cries, and, though Jesus did give His life, He was raised! The prayers of our great High Priest were received by the Father, they were effective, and Jesus was rescued by the only one who was able to save Him from death.

Today, when we pray, we don't go to God according to our own authority. We may never meet the world's great historical figures, or even influential people alive today. However, we are invited to come into God's presence—Jesus is our High Priest and He's happy to bring us into the presence of the Father. And when we pray through Christ, we can have confidence that, just as the Father heard Jesus' prayers in the garden, He will receive Jesus' prayers on our behalf as well.

When do you feel unfit to come into the presence of God?

We are unfit to approach God because of our sin. How are we able to come before God?

Why can you trust that God receives your prayers, and they actually make a difference?

PRAY WITH JESUS

Father, I recognize that there's no reason I should have the privilege of coming into Your presence, except that You love me and give me grace because of Jesus.

JOURNAL YOUR OWN PRAYER:

"Now my soul is troubled. What should I say—Father, save me from this hour? But that is why I came to this hour. Father, glorify your name." Then a voice came from heaven: "I have glorified it, and I will glorify it again." **JOHN 12:27-28**

When I was in college, I played in a band that had the opportunity to travel nationwide. I found out that the day-in, day-out reality was not nearly as romantic as I'd imagined before. However, I have to be honest—traveling to different places, making records, eating every city's best food, meeting so many great people, and creating music every day was a pretty good time. However, I'd regularly run up against what I call "dark-cloud moments." On a Sunday, we'd wrap up a weekend retreat. We'd have experienced amazing worship, been under the teaching of an inspiring teacher, and leave incredibly encouraged by the ways God had used us to impact people's lives. Then I'd remember my statistics test the following morning, for which I was drastically underprepared! The rest of the trip home was colored by the dark cloud hanging over me, and I wasn't free to enjoy what would otherwise have been an amazing experience.

As Jesus neared the end of His earthly ministry, He'd become a household name throughout the entire region. When Jesus taught in the synagogues, He spoke with authority unlike anyone had ever heard, and people had come to recognize Him as an incredible teacher. When the sick, having exhausted every other possibility for healing, came to Jesus, He showed compassion and miraculously healed many, many people. He'd demonstrated His divine nature through multiplying food and commanding nature. The people had also heard about His raising Lazarus from the dead, and, one way or another, everyone was talking about Jesus.

When the week of Jesus' final Passover came, as happened every year, faithful Jews from all across Israel traveled to Jerusalem to participate in the feast. As Jesus entered the city on the back of a donkey's colt, multitudes came out to greet Him, exclaiming, "Hosanna! Blessed is he who comes in the name of the Lord!" (Mark 11:9b). To this point, though Jesus had pointed to the fact that He was God's chosen Messiah, He hadn't yet made a bold and public declaration—it would likely have resulted in His arrest and crucifixion before His time had come. At His triumphal entry, however, His time had finally come, and He basically made the claim before all Israel—"I am God's Deliverer."

The Jews had waited for generations for Jesus, and they greeted Him with fanfare, lavishing praise on the Lord's chosen one. However, despite such a royal welcome and what appears to be reason for Jesus to be extraordinarily encouraged, there was a dark cloud—one far darker than anything we'll ever experience—looming, and Jesus simply couldn't shake it.

As Jesus was talking with His disciples, teaching them a few final lessons that were imperative they understand before His departure, He shared with them the internal anguish He was experiencing. Jesus stated simply, "My soul is troubled" (v. 27). Jesus is, of course, fully God, but He is also fully man, and in His humanity, Jesus was deeply distressed at the thought of the cross. He'd not only suffer unimaginable physical pain, He'd endure God's wrath upon sin.

However, despite feeling this way, Jesus understood very clearly the purpose for which He was sent to earth. And He was wholeheartedly committed to that. So He asked, "What should I say—Father, save me from this hour?" (v. 27).

In a matter of days, He would ask that very thing. Jesus would basically pray in the garden, *Father, if You're willing, please spare me from this experience.* Yet, even in this request showed a special kind of humility that yielded completely to the will of the Father. Before praying, Jesus knew His purpose and He knew the Father's answer. Yet He was free to openly express His heart, for He had positioned Himself in wholehearted submission before the Father.

Today, it's important that we understand God welcomes the honest prayers of His children, even when our desires are not perfectly conformed to His will. As long as we approach Him humbly, God can use all our prayers to bring us to a deeper dependence upon Him and a clearer understanding of His purposes in our lives.

When have you struggled with accepting what you knew to be God's will for your life?

What steps did you take to conform your heart to God's?

How can you work to balance praying honestly with praying for God's will?

PRAY WITH JESUS

Father, thank You for receiving my prayers, even when they reveal my weaknesses and lack of eternal perspective. Help me to be continually humble before You, and to have a healthy eternal perspective on all things.

JOURNAL YOUR OWN PRAYER:

Session 8
DURING SUFFERING

Focal Passage // Luke 23:33-34,46

Memory Verse // Hebrews 12:2

Keeping our eyes on Jesus, the source and perfecter of our faith. For the joy that lay before him, he endured the cross, despising the shame, and sat down at the right hand of the throne of God.

Weekly Reading // Luke 23:1-24:53

We live in a world where it's sometimes hard to trust people. The news is full of stories of accusations that bring utter devastation to the lives of the accused—and who even knows if what's being said is true or not? We hear more days than not of betrayals that ruin relationships, divide families, and inflict unimaginable pain on people from all walks of life. Chances are, we've all experienced something along these lines. Perhaps...

- A friend turned out to be a "mean girl" and shared your secrets with the whole class.
- Someone you were once close to fell in with the "cool kids" and started making fun of you.
- Your parents—those responsible to take care of you no matter what—did something to disappoint or hurt you.

Describe a time someone you trusted let you down.

To experience the sort of intimacy for which God designed us, we have to be willing to open up and be vulnerable with others. This isn't to say we should trust in anyone and everyone. We're to take great care, exercising wisdom with something this precious. However, at some point, we must be willing to make the leap.

The intimacy and trust between Jesus and the Father are unique in all of history. The Father entrusted Jesus with the great responsibility of redeeming humanity, and Jesus, in the most vulnerable moment ever experienced by any human, literally put His life in the Father's hands.

Every one of us is going to make a decision about who controls our lives. If we're wise, we'll trust our parents. Though they're not perfect, they love us and have a lot of wisdom due to life experience. We'd all do well to find godly friends and invite them into our lives for encouragement and accountability. And of course it's wise to do all we can to grow in godliness so that, on a healthy level, we can trust ourselves to make right decisions. However, above all these, we need to trust God. The same one who could lead and support Jesus through literally taking on the sin of the world says to us, *I love you. I'll take care of you. Give your life to me!*

Watch this session's video, and then continue to the group discussion section using the content provided.

THEY CRUCIFIED HIM THERE

From before the foundation of the world, it was God's plan that Jesus would be crucified for the sin of mankind (1 Pet. 1:18-20). Sometimes it's easy for us to focus on God's transcendence—that He's different from and far above us—and lose sight of the fact that Jesus lived as a real man. Despite that Jesus is eternal, He experienced life in real-time in the real world, just like us. When Jesus ate fish off the fire, it was delicious! When He hugged His mom, His emotions swelled from the warmth and acceptance that only a mother can give. On the other hand, as He drew nearer and nearer to the cross, Jesus felt the worry intensify. As He faced trials before earthly leaders, He faced the corruption of earthly injustice. And as the nails were driven into His hands and feet, His nerves screamed with fiery pain.

If you're anything like me, when things get tough, we tend to treat others in ways that are less than kind. When we get a little tired, we become edgy. If others get on our nerves, we can be downright mean. Imagine how we'd be tempted to respond if we experienced the kind of suffering Jesus faced. How do you treat others when you're in a bad mood?

Let's take a look at how Jesus ended up here. He left heaven, lived a sinless life, and loved people perfectly. Jesus fed those who were hungry, healed countless people who were suffering, and delivered those oppressed by demons. And perhaps most importantly, He shared with anyone who would listen to the truth about how we can live in relationship with God. Despite all of this, the world hated Him and sentenced Him to death on a cross.

When we suffer, it's often because of our own bad choices. And we still get mad (even though we deserve bad things). But Jesus deserved none of the suffering He received, and still, He responded with love and grace. As if He hadn't done so already, in the midst of the worst suffering imaginable, Jesus demonstrated the true condition of His heart. Instead of calling down curses upon His murderers, He prayed for the very people who put Him on the cross. Jesus had earlier taught that we are to love our enemies (Matt. 5:44), and now He was providing an example in the ultimate sense.

In this world, we will face suffering (John 16:33), often at the hands of those who are opposed to God, and us! Prayer is an important part of responding well—loving others, even those who hate us—in our suffering.

When have you suffered when you didn't deserve it? How did your response serve as a reflection of God's power and love?

FATHER FORGIVE THEM

Self-control is listed among the fruit of the Spirit (Gal. 5:22-23), and although all believers have it, we don't always exercise it. Let's do a little test. Girls, when your little brother follows you around, mimicking your voice for the 827th time today, how do you respond? Guys, when your little sister has decided to practice her marker skills on your new shoes, how do you speak to her? We know how we should respond in these situations, but that's not always how it works out.

Exercising self-control has not only to do with the ways we act externally, but also with our internal responses, especially to difficult situations. Often, when people do things that get on our nerves, or if they treat us in ways that are particularly offensive, we let our emotions get the best of us, we lose our temper, and we act in ways that are a bit out of control. We make excuses like, "that wasn't really me"—except that it really was. Our words, in fact, our whole lives, flow out of our hearts (Matt. 12:34; Prov. 27:19). So the truth is that our actions reveal our character, and when we're tested, we can know all the more clearly who we are deep down.

As Jesus hung on the cross, the worst was yet to come. By the nails, the thorns, and the spear, He suffered unimaginable physical pain, but He was yet to endure the spiritual torment associated with being relationally cut off from the Father and enduring the punishment for the sin of the world. And as He anticipated this, because of His perfect love for the lost, even as they mocked Him and gambled for His clothes, He prayed for sinners—"Father, forgive them, because they do not know what they are doing" (Luke 23:34).

Jesus prayed most immediately for the Roman soldiers who had held the hammers and nails. More broadly, however, the prayer applied to all those who put Jesus on the cross—Israel's religious leaders, the Jewish people, even you and me! Jesus didn't pray this way because He knew it was the right thing or because He needed to check the pray-for-others block before He died. He prayed because He had such a deep love for people and a profound passion for the lost. There was nothing else He'd rather have done in that moment. It was an expression of His heart. And we can be certain that Jesus' prayer was effective in bringing many to faith in Him.

None of us will ever face the kind of trial Jesus faced on the cross. But we will, one way or the other, face trials in this life. It may be legitimate persecution, or it may be that we endure the effects of sin in this world. Either way, we are called to demonstrate the heart of Christ in our trials, and when we endure well, we have a great opportunity to show the difference Jesus makes in our lives. Instead of focusing on ourselves and becoming nasty or hateful, let's pray that God would strengthen us to endure, and that He would use our suffering to open others' eyes to the truth of the gospel.

How has God used hardships you've faced to help others see Christ's love in you?

INTO YOUR HANDS

Recently, I had to go into the hospital for the first time, and my 39-year-run of hospital-free living came to its abrupt conclusion. I'm not generally a fearful person. In fact, I think most people who know me would say that I'm pretty bold, even fearless (this is not always a good thing). But as I was about to go under for surgery, I was pretty nervous. After all, I was putting my life into the hands of a surgeon I didn't know very well. Sure, he was well qualified (at least I assume he was ... he never showed me his diplomas), but even the best surgeons make mistakes. Describe a time when you put your life in someone else's hands.

To be a Christian means fully surrendering our lives to God. Yet sometimes, though we've sung songs such as "I Surrender All," and we say things like I've given my life (my whole life) to Jesus, we like to take back certain areas. We're happy to give God everything—except:

- **Entertainment:** Surely God won't be mad if I listen to music or watch movies with just a little bad stuff.
- **Romantic relationships:** We don't go too far, so I guess it's alright.
- **Time:** As long as I go to church every week, I'm free to do what I want the rest of the time.
- **Money:** I don't have much, so I have to spend what I do have on the things I need.

For Jesus, surrendering to God meant laying more on the line than we could ever imagine. When He left heaven and came to earth, He gave up more than we can even begin to appreciate. When He went to the cross, unimaginable suffering awaited Him there. And as He approached death, the cost of surrender was the highest price tag in history. Jesus could have called on His Father for rescue (Matt. 26:53). He could have summoned an army of angels to exercise judgment on those who had mistreated Him (By the way, 2 Kin. 19:35 teaches that a single angel easily killed 185,000 soldiers. Imagine the force of 72,000 angels!). But because the Father had a plan that didn't include these things, Jesus willingly surrendered in the fullest sense. After hanging on the cross for six hours, and with a supernatural darkness covering the face of the earth, Jesus cried out, "Father, into your hands I entrust my spirit."

For Christians, coming to faith required that, at some point, we prayed the same prayer— *Father, I surrender my life to You.* Yet we don't always continue living this way as we should. Jesus' life was a continual expression of surrender to the Father, and to pray like Jesus means, moment by moment, with every choice and every thought, placing our lives in the hands of the Father.

What is God calling you to surrender to Him today?

1. They Crucified Him There

Throughout Jesus' ministry, He faced the worst kinds of resistance and rejection. But through it all, He treated people with patience and love. Even when He was on the cross, He felt compassion for those whose lives were captured by sin.

When have you felt compassion for those who have wronged you?

How can you demonstrate the love of Christ to those who treat you unkindly?

2. Father Forgive Them

We aren't supposed to live the way we should as a matter of obligation, but from the heart. Jesus didn't pray for those who crucified Him because He knew He was "supposed" to. He prayed because of His deep love for people.

What in your life demonstrates this kind of love for people? This kind of grief over sin?

How can prayer help you to cultivate genuine love and compassion toward all people?

3. Into Your Hands

We often have trouble trusting others openly, and the idea of fully surrendering to God can make us uneasy. However, God is faithful, He is powerful, and He is working everything for the good of those who love Him and who devote our lives to His purposes.

What does your life show about the ways you trust others?

What would it look like to fully place your life into God's hands? How can prayer help you to take this step?

PRAY LIKE JESUS

Take a few minutes right now to pray for these things. Make it a point to pray:

- That God would help you to show kindness to others, especially when you're facing hard things
- That God would give you a heart of love and compassion toward those who treat you unkindly
- That God would help you live in full surrender to Him every moment of your life

Then I will pour out a spirit of grace and prayer on the house of David and the residents of Jerusalem, and they will look at me whom they pierced. They will mourn for him as one mourns for an only child and weep bitterly for him as one weeps for a firstborn.
ZECHARIAH 12:10

Regret can be a tough burden to bear. In fact, it's not uncommon for people, rather than owning their mistakes and allowing themselves to experience remorse, to take a more defensive position—*sure, I've made mistakes, but I wouldn't change a thing because it's made me who I am.* On the surface, this sounds okay. However, when we think about it, it's a pretty selfish perspective which is concerned only with ourselves, and with no regard for how our mistakes and misbehaviors have injured others along the way. And honestly, it's hard to imagine how a past full of slip-ups and selfishness leads to a better self than if we'd have had our lives shaped by conformity to God's law.

Israel experienced their fair share of failure throughout the generations. And the consequences they experienced as a result led to some deep regret. No matter how hard-hearted the Israelites became, and despite having many of God's blessings removed, the Lord was faithful over and over again to send messages through the prophets reminding them of His great love. The people would experience regret—if not over their sin, at least because of the consequences—and they would return to God. However, at a certain point in history, God's people had turned away from Him, and despite that God called repeatedly for His people to return, they'd become so hardened to spiritual things that they altogether rejected God's prophecy. God's response was to quit speaking, and for 400 years, God's people wouldn't receive even one word from the Lord.

However, before God uttered those final Old Testament words, He sent a promise through Zechariah: "I will pour out a spirit of grace and prayer on the house of David and the residents of Jerusalem, and they will look at me whom they pierced. They will mourn…"

Israel had committed the worst kinds of offenses against the God who had shown them infinite kindness. He had kindly revealed Himself to them, and they turned to idols. He had given them the law, and they ignored His commands. He had set His love on them, and they instead loved the world. Yet, just as when they'd been slaves in Egypt and cried out in their suffering, after hundreds of years of separation, God graciously chose to give good gifts once again to His people. Though Jerusalem didn't have eyes to see who Jesus was while He was on earth, God allowed them soon after to see clearly who Jesus is, and themselves in light of the glory of Christ.

Throughout their history, Israel was forced multiple times to own up to their rebellion against God, and when they rejected His Son, they came face-to-face with their ultimate sin. They could have been defensive, making excuses and hardening their hearts as they'd done so many times before. However, because God poured out a spirit of grace and prayer, they responded exactly as they should have—with deep regret. God's grace produced godly sorrow in the hearts of His people, which moved them to prayerful confession and repentance, and through this, God restored His people.

Many people today are quite familiar with Jesus, even to the point of calling themselves Christians, yet they fail to live as Jesus lived. Just like Israel, they see themselves as God's people. However, because Jesus is holy and we are desperately sinful, if knowing Jesus produces anything other than prayer and repentance, we haven't seen Jesus as He truly is. Yet when we do repent and pray as a result of knowing Jesus, God is happy to bless us with the greatest gift—knowing Him.

When have you seen Jesus but failed to live in light of who He is?

How has God caused you to mourn over your sin?

How have you seen God create a spirit of prayer and repentance in you?

PRAY WITH JESUS

Father, I confess that there have been times I've sinned against You, and instead of owning it, I've made excuses. Thank You for being patient with me when I've lived this way, and for convicting me of my sins so that I could be restored to a relationship with You.

JOURNAL YOUR OWN PRAYER:

DEVO // DAY 2

I called to the LORD in distress; the LORD answered me and put me in a spacious place. The LORD is for me; I will not be afraid. What can a mere mortal do to me? The LORD is my helper, Therefore, I will look in triumph on those who hate me. **PSALM 118:5-7**

Stress. This is something most people experience fairly regularly. If the game is on the line, and you know the ball is coming your way—stress. Sadness. We all, from time to time, experience things that make us sad. When a good friend we've known for years moves away to another state—sadness. But distress isn't nearly as common an experience. It means "extreme" anxiety, sorrow or pain, and though (thankfully) it doesn't rear it's head too often in our lives, there will certainly be times we'll face real distress.

In Psalm 118, we read the words of a writer who knew what it was like to face the most difficult of circumstances. Though scholars can't say definitively who wrote this psalm, it's likely Moses who wrote it, as we see much of the language from Exodus 15 (which was written by Moses) is repeated in Psalm 118:

- **Exodus 15:2**—"The LORD is my strength and my song; he has become my salvation. This is my God, and I will praise him, my father's God, and I will exalt him."
- **Psalm 118:14**—"The LORD is my strength and my song; he has become my salvation."
- **Exodus 15:6,12**—"LORD, your right hand is glorious in power. LORD, your right hand shattered the enemy ... You stretched out your right hand, and the earth swallowed them."
- **Psalm 118:15-16**—"There are shouts of joy and victory in the tents of the righteous: 'The LORD's right hand performs valiantly! The LORD's right hand is raised. The LORD's right hand performs valiantly!'"
- **Psalm 118:28**—"You are my God, and I will give you thanks. You are my God; I will exalt you."

Moses knew what it was to experience hard things. When he was a baby, Egypt's pharaoh had ordered all the baby boys be killed. Years later, Moses made some bad choices and had to flee his home for fear of his life. God then called Moses to lead His people, and they were a stubborn bunch who continually complained, argued, and rebelled. Then there was the matter of being stuck in the desert, including not knowing at times where food and water would come from, the continual threat of hostile tribes, and having no home. Any one of these would be enough to cause us great distress. Moses had all these stacked on top of one another, and the trouble and worry he faced was compounded in ways that are hard to imagine.

Yet, Moses had experienced God's great love in real ways throughout His life. As a baby, his life had been spared in an incredible way. When Moses sinned, God protected him from Pharaoh's wrath. When the people complained and rebelled, God instructed Moses as to how to lead them. When God's people were in the desert, Moses got to witness God providing food and water, fighting for His people, and leading them step-by-step toward the land He had promised them. And through all the trouble, Moses learned an important lesson.

When we experience the worst that life has to throw at us, we're free to cry out to God, and He receives our prayers. And through it all, Moses learned to trust God completely.

When we experience difficulties, either because of personal sin or due to sin's curse upon creation, in a certain sense, we get what we deserve. However, the suffering Jesus endured was not only the worst possible agony, but it was also totally undeserved. Nonetheless, Jesus cried out to God in prayer, He committed His spirit into the hands of His Father, and God answered. God wouldn't allow Jesus to remain in death, but He raised Him in victory over death. When we cry out in distress, and from the place of total trust in God, we can expect God will answer us as well.

When has God used trouble in your life to help you trust Him more?

Why are we more likely to pray when life is difficult?

What "distress" are you currently facing to which you should respond with prayer?

PRAY WITH JESUS

Father, I'm thankful that, through the hard times in my life, You've helped me to learn to trust You more. Help me to respond in prayer to all that brings me distress, and help me to recognize the ways You answer.

JOURNAL YOUR OWN PRAYER:

"While they were stoning Stephen, he called out: 'Lord Jesus, receive my spirit!' He knelt down and cried out with a loud voice, 'Lord, do not hold this sin against them!' And after saying this, he died." **ACTS 7:59-60**

As the young church grew, the apostles who had the responsibility of overseeing the church had trouble keeping up with the growing demands (Acts 6:1). On one particular occasion, an argument made it very clear to the church's leaders that they needed a new plan. So they had the people choose a leader who would handle a large portion of the daily responsibilities so the apostles could focus on teaching Scripture and prayer. The qualifications for the new servants were that they have a good reputation, possess great wisdom, and be full of the Spirit. Stephen was one of the men chosen for this position, and he did a great job! In fact, as Stephen committed himself to doing exactly what God had called him to do, the Holy Spirit used him to demonstrate God's goodness in powerful ways to the people.

However, not everyone was thrilled with Stephen, and they were offended by the message of Jesus he continually taught. They tried to debate Stephen, but, as the Spirit spoke through him, they were utterly humiliated, and decided to trump up false accusations to get even. Word made it to the Jewish leaders, and Stephen was arrested and taken before the Sanhedrin, which was essentially the Jewish supreme court. They basically asked him, *Is it true that you've spoken blasphemy against Moses and against God? Are you claiming that Jesus came to destroy the temple and its customs?*

In answering, though faced with the most difficult of circumstances, Stephen never shrunk back from speaking the gospel. He recounted God's calling of Abraham, how God had worked to establish Israel through their forefathers, and how He had delivered the law through Moses. Stephen also reminded the judges and the people who were looking on of how Israel had rejected Moses. He then pointed out that Moses had predicted God would send a Deliverer like himself, and that Israel would reject that prophet as well.

All who heard this were enraged, and as they dragged Stephen outside of the city to stone him—the prescribed penalty for blasphemy—Stephen never wavered from his devotion to God, even in his dying moments. As the stones crashed against his body, Stephen lifted his eyes, and had a vision of Jesus in the presence of God and the heavens opened to receive him. With his final breaths, Stephen, who understood what it meant to live like Jesus, chose also to die in a manner similar to his Lord—praying. He called out to Jesus:

- **"Receive my spirit!"**—Had Stephen set his heart on earthly things, he would have made much different choices. However, he loved God so much and was so clearly focused on eternity that his experience in an earthly sense paled in comparison. As Jesus died, He prayed, "Father, into your hands I entrust my spirit," and Stephen was so fully in tune with his Savior, his natural expression during his dying moments expressed the same kind of trust in God.

- **"Do not hold this sin against them!"**—The nature of true love is to be willing to sacrifice for the good of others. As Stephen died unfairly at the hands of those who hated him, the natural response of many would have been anger or despair. However, Stephen didn't respond according to the old nature, but to the new nature that results from being born again. There wasn't even a hint of selfishness in Stephen's response, but, just like Jesus' prayer from the cross, the expressed desire for those who had set themselves against God was to know His forgiveness.

We know, as followers of Christ, we're called to be like Him. However, it sometimes seems out of reach—after all, He's perfect and we're not! Thankfully, we have record of regular people, just like you and me, living in ways that clearly reflect the love of Jesus in even the most difficult of circumstances. Stephen was a man full of wisdom and the Holy Spirit, and in his final moments, he chose to pray as an expression of his trust in God and his love for people. Let's devote ourselves to prayer in the same ways, not just in our dying moments, but in our living moments as well.

When are you tempted to respond to unkindness differently than Stephen?

What do you think brought Stephen to the place that he responded as he did?

How can you grow as you seek to respond in Christ-like ways?

PRAY WITH JESUS

Father, I understand that because the world is broken by sin, and that I will experience hardship and will be treated unfairly at times. Help me to respond as Stephen did—with complete trust in You and with love for even those who treat me unkindly.

> **JOURNAL YOUR OWN PRAYER:**

"Therefore, he is able to save completely those who come to God through him, since he always lives to intercede for them." **HEBREWS 7:25**

Most schools in American grade on a 10-point scale. Ninety to 100 is an A, 80 to 89 is a B, and so on. This is how it worked for me throughout high school, however, later in my education, I discovered that my school didn't grade according to a 10-point window. The scale was 7 points instead—an A was 93 and above, and to get a passing C, a 77 was required. This higher standard wasn't necessarily preferable as far as I was concerned. The more rigorous expectations supposedly holds students to a higher level of accountability, motivates harder work and more thorough preparation, and communicates something about the schools standards. For me, I'd rather have had a 10-point scale.

Despite this new paradigm's being a little tough to get used to, the worst was yet to come. From time to time, certain professors structured their classes such that assignments along the way were purely for learning—and not for grades—and whether or not students passed the class depended entirely on the final exam. We had one chance to get it right, and we had to make the most of that one-test opportunity. What I found was that many students, because weekly assignments weren't for grades, would skip class and ignore assignments, expecting to live the good life for 15 weeks and cram the last few days before the final.

It's one thing to approach a college class this way. However, it's an altogether different reality to view life this way. There are many people who recognize their need for God in their lives. However, much like completing weekly assignments, they see God's commands as a checklist that simply cramps their style. They want to be free to do whatever they'd like, and then one day—when the time is right, at least in their minds—they'll catch up on doing all the right things and they'll get in line with God.

This simply isn't the way it works. We don't work to complete "assignments," as if God's handing out daily grades, and if we've met a certain number on the scale, we have the privilege of passing on into heaven. Receiving God's blessing and living in His presence is not a matter of tipping the scales in our favor by being a "good" person, as if 51 percent makes us fit for heaven. It's not about working hard our whole lives to earn 70 percent, or even 90 percent approval. God's standard is pass-fail, but even then, it's far higher than any college class could ever require. God is holy, His standard is absolute perfection, and this is something we could never earn ourselves. But Jesus did, and He wants to share His good-standing before God with us.

Jesus went to the cross in order to reconcile us to God. In fact, His passing the test is the only way to God, and even though He wanted to avoid the suffering of the cross, He was more concerned with the Father's will and the welfare of sinners than He was about Himself. This is why He prayed the ways He did on the cross, and His prayers are infinitely valuable in the lives of those God saves.

Jesus' prayers play a necessary part in our salvation. Because our sin separates us from God, we can't come into His presence, so Jesus prays for us. Further, when there was no way for us to meet God's standard, Jesus paid the cost so that we could be saved. Not just mostly saved—saved completely. To the fullest extent. One hundred percent!

Because of Jesus' perfect life, because He died and was raised, and because He prays for us, we can have confidence in our standing before God. Out of this, we are called, like Jesus, to love others sacrificially and pray for them that they would find approval in Jesus as well.

When have you felt like you could never meet God's standard to go to heaven? By contrast, when have you felt like you were "good enough" to be part of God's family?

What difference does it make that Jesus lives to intercede for God's people, and that He saves us completely?

How can you live to intercede for the lost that they would receive the approval of God?

PRAY WITH JESUS

Father, I understand very clearly that I could never live up to your perfect standard, and that Jesus is the only one who ever could. Thank You for sending Jesus to intercede for Your people, and ultimately to make us fit for heaven.

JOURNAL YOUR OWN PRAYER:

"But I say to you who listen: Love your enemies, do what is good to those who hate you, bless those who curse you, pray for those who mistreat you." **LUKE 6:27-28**

There are certain words in our language that stand out as particularly strong, and when they're used, they can grab our attention. Some are positive. Of course, there's *love*. But there are many others. For instance, *fantastic* refers to something unimaginably good, that seems to good to be true, that must the object of fantasy. Some strong words, on the other hand, are quite negative. *Atrocious* doesn't mean just bad, but horrifyingly terrible. Someone who's *wicked* isn't just mean, they're purely evil. Jesus used words like these, not only to grab the attention of His hearers, but also in order to make bold points about the nature of the kingdom.

Jesus stated that His followers will love our enemies, and do good to those who live hatefully toward us. To most people, this is unimaginable. From the world's perspective, it's appropriate to do good to those who are kind to us. Some even to make sacrifices for loved ones. But Christians are called to an entirely different standard, for it's through this difference the power of God is made known in our lives. If we simply do what the world does—love those who love us—what difference does it make, really?

The standard Jesus set for His followers is not just to do to others as they've done to us, but also to treat all people how we want to be treated, regardless of how they've treated us. So, when I make a mistake, I have to ask myself, *How would I want others to treat me? With harsh judgment? Highly critically? To put me down and let me know what a failure I am?* No way, I want people to be patient with me, and even to help me learn to do better in the future. This is how I should treat others. When I choose to live hurtfully toward others, I must ask, *How would I want them to respond? Do I want them to write me off forever? Send their big brother over to beat me up?* No, I'd want them to show me grace, and to be willing to forgive me.

When others act hurtfully to us, it's often easy to take it personally. However, it's important for us to understand that people often act out of a place of hurt themselves. They experience pain in their lives, and they don't have the coping skills or the information necessary to deal with it well. Even beyond the relational reality is the fact that, ultimately, our conflict isn't with other people, rather our struggle is a spiritual one (Eph. 6:12).

When our natural response is to fight back, an eye for an eye with those who do us harm, it never accomplishes anything good for the name of Jesus. However, when we suffer, and instead of responding in turn, we choose to do good to those who've hated us—to show love to our enemies—God has a way of using our choices to help others see the difference He makes in the lives of His people. And one of the best ways we can make sure to live this out is to seek the blessings of those who have set themselves against us, praying continually God would work in their hearts.

Again, this can be a struggle. The natural response toward people who treat us badly is to desire they'd experience bad things too. But this isn't the way of Jesus. Toward those who committed the ultimate wrong against Him, they put Him on the cross to die. Jesus had no ill will, no anger, no hatred, no desire for violence—only compassion. Toward His enemies (strong word meaning "violently opposed"), toward those who hated Him (strong word meaning "intense loathing"), He chose to pray for them as an expression of His desire for their ultimate good.

Because of our sin, we were Jesus' enemies. But He prayed for us. He gave His life for us! Since Jesus' prayers and sacrifice are effective, we are now part of God's family. Included in our call to be like Jesus is our responsibility to do the same things—to love others, even those who hate us, and to pray for the good of all people. As we reflect Christ's love by living in ways that are unnatural to worldly people, but are altogether natural for those who are born of the Spirit, God will likewise use our prayers, sacrifices, and love for others to make a difference in others' lives. This is why we were created. Let's be like Jesus.

When have others treated you unkindly? How did you respond?

Why is it sometimes difficult to love those who hate us?

How can praying for your enemies help you to see others as Jesus does?

PRAY WITH JESUS

Father, I understand that, because of my sin, I was Your enemy. Yet You chose to love me anyway. Thank You! Please work in my heart to help me to love others in the same ways. Help me to reflect Jesus in the ways I desire and do good to all people.

JOURNAL YOUR OWN PRAYER:

Leader
GUIDE

Engage

Use this introduction as a way to begin your group time before watching the session video.

Watch

Watch the video for Session 1 (included in the DVD Kit). Allow students time to ask any clarifying questions about the video before continuing to the Group Discussion section using the content provided.

Group Discussion

Use the Group Discussion pages to guide your group through an in-depth discussion of the relevant biblical passages for this session. Adding to the video content, the Group Discussion section will provide additional insight and clarification into key biblical concepts as students work through the session content.

Prayer in Real Life

As a group, work through the application section that follows the Group Discussion. The application section ends with a call to prayer that is specific to the content of that session, as well as an opportunity for students to write a personal prayer based on what they have learned throughout the lesson. Allow students some time to complete these personal prayers in the space provided and then transition to a time of corporate prayer to close out your time as a group.

Weekly Leader Tips

- Introduce the personal devotions that follow each session and remind students to complete Session 1 devotions before your next meeting.

- Encourage students to memorize Session 1 memory verse this week.

- Challenge students to be in the habit of building into their own personal prayer lives what they have learned this week.

LEADER GUIDE // SESSION 2

Engage

Use this introduction as a way to begin your group time before watching the session video.

Watch

Watch the video for Session 2 (included in the DVD Kit). Allow students time to ask any clarifying questions about the video before continuing to the Group Discussion section using the content provided.

Group Discussion

Use the Group Discussion pages to guide your group through an in-depth discussion of the relevant biblical passages for this session. Adding to the video content, the Group Discussion section will provide additional insight and clarification into key biblical concepts as students work through the session content.

Prayer in Real Life

As a group, work through the application section that follows the Group Discussion. The application section ends with a call to prayer that is specific to the content of that session, as well as an opportunity for students to write a personal prayer based on what they have learned throughout the lesson. Allow students some time to complete these personal prayers in the space provided and then transition to a time of corporate prayer to close out your time as a group.

Weekly Leader Tips

- Remind students about the personal devotions and to complete Session 2 devotions before your next meeting.

- Encourage students to memorize Session 2 memory verse this week.

- Challenge students to be in the habit of building into their own personal prayer lives what they have learned this week.

Engage

Use this introduction as a way to begin your group time before watching the session video.

Watch

Watch the video for Session 3 (included in the DVD Kit). Allow students time to ask any clarifying questions about the video before continuing to the Group Discussion section using the content provided.

Group Discussion

Use the Group Discussion pages to guide your group through an in-depth discussion of the relevant biblical passages for this session. Adding to the video content, the Group Discussion section will provide additional insight and clarification into key biblical concepts as students work through the session content.

Prayer in Real Life

As a group, work through the application section that follows the Group Discussion. The application section ends with a call to prayer that is specific to the content of that session, as well as an opportunity for students to write a personal prayer based on what they have learned throughout the lesson. Allow students some time to complete these personal prayers in the space provided and then transition to a time of corporate prayer to close out your time as a group.

Weekly Leader Tips

- Remind students about the personal devotions and to complete Session 3 devotions before your next meeting.

- Encourage students to memorize Session 3 memory verse this week.

- Challenge students to be in the habit of building into their own personal prayer lives what they have learned this week.

LEADER GUIDE // SESSION 4

Engage

Use this introduction as a way to begin your group time before watching the session video.

Watch

Watch the video for Session 4 (included in the DVD Kit). Allow students time to ask any clarifying questions about the video before continuing to the Group Discussion section using the content provided.

Group Discussion

Use the Group Discussion pages to guide your group through an in-depth discussion of the relevant biblical passages for this session. Adding to the video content, the Group Discussion section will provide additional insight and clarification into key biblical concepts as students work through the session content.

Prayer in Real Life

As a group, work through the application section that follows the Group Discussion. The application section ends with a call to prayer that is specific to the content of that session, as well as an opportunity for students to write a personal prayer based on what they have learned throughout the lesson. Allow students some time to complete these personal prayers in the space provided and then transition to a time of corporate prayer to close out your time as a group.

Weekly Leader Tips

- Remind students about the personal devotions and to complete Session 4 devotions before your next meeting.

- Encourage students to memorize Session 4 memory verse this week.

- Challenge students to be in the habit of building into their own personal prayer lives what they have learned this week.

Engage

Use this introduction as a way to begin your group time before watching the session video.

Watch

Watch the video for Session 5 (included in the DVD Kit). Allow students time to ask any clarifying questions about the video before continuing to the Group Discussion section using the content provided.

Group Discussion

Use the Group Discussion pages to guide your group through an in-depth discussion of the relevant biblical passages for this session. Adding to the video content, the Group Discussion section will provide additional insight and clarification into key biblical concepts as students work through the session content.

Prayer in Real Life

As a group, work through the application section that follows the Group Discussion. The application section ends with a call to prayer that is specific to the content of that session, as well as an opportunity for students to write a personal prayer based on what they have learned throughout the lesson. Allow students some time to complete these personal prayers in the space provided and then transition to a time of corporate prayer to close out your time as a group.

Weekly Leader Tips

- Remind students about the personal devotions and to complete Session 5 devotions before your next meeting.

- Encourage students to memorize Session 5 memory verse this week.

- Challenge students to be in the habit of building into their own personal prayer lives what they have learned this week.

LEADER GUIDE // SESSION 6

Engage

Use this introduction as a way to begin your group time before watching the session video.

Watch

Watch the video for Session 6 (included in the DVD Kit). Allow students time to ask any clarifying questions about the video before continuing to the Group Discussion section using the content provided.

Group Discussion

Use the Group Discussion pages to guide your group through an in-depth discussion of the relevant biblical passages for this session. Adding to the video content, the Group Discussion section will provide additional insight and clarification into key biblical concepts as students work through the session content.

Prayer in Real Life

As a group, work through the application section that follows the Group Discussion. The application section ends with a call to prayer that is specific to the content of that session, as well as an opportunity for students to write a personal prayer based on what they have learned throughout the lesson. Allow students some time to complete these personal prayers in the space provided and then transition to a time of corporate prayer to close out your time as a group.

Weekly Leader Tips

- Remind students about the personal devotions and to complete Session 6 devotions before your next meeting.

- Encourage students to memorize Session 6 memory verse this week.

- Challenge students to be in the habit of building into their own personal prayer lives what they have learned this week.

Engage

Use this introduction as a way to begin your group time before watching the session video.

Watch

Watch the video for Session 7 (included in the DVD Kit). Allow students time to ask any clarifying questions about the video before continuing to the Group Discussion section using the content provided.

Group Discussion

Use the Group Discussion pages to guide your group through an in-depth discussion of the relevant biblical passages for this session. Adding to the video content, the Group Discussion section will provide additional insight and clarification into key biblical concepts as students work through the session content.

Prayer in Real Life

As a group, work through the application section that follows the Group Discussion. The application section ends with a call to prayer that is specific to the content of that session, as well as an opportunity for students to write a personal prayer based on what they have learned throughout the lesson. Allow students some time to complete these personal prayers in the space provided and then transition to a time of corporate prayer to close out your time as a group.

Weekly Leader Tips

- Remind students about the personal devotions and to complete Session 7 devotions before your next meeting.

- Encourage students to memorize Session 7 memory verse this week.

- Challenge students to be in the habit of building into their own personal prayer lives what they have learned this week.

LEADER GUIDE // SESSION 8

Engage

Use this introduction as a way to begin your group time before watching the session video.

Watch

Watch the video for Session 8 (included in the DVD Kit). Allow students time to ask any clarifying questions about the video before continuing to the Group Discussion section using the content provided.

Group Discussion

Use the Group Discussion pages to guide your group through an in-depth discussion of the relevant biblical passages for this session. Adding to the video content, the Group Discussion section will provide additional insight and clarification into key biblical concepts as students work through the session content.

Prayer in Real Life

As a group, work through the application section that follows the Group Discussion. The application section ends with a call to prayer that is specific to the content of that session, as well as an opportunity for students to write a personal prayer based on what they have learned throughout the lesson. Allow students some time to complete these personal prayers in the space provided and then transition to a time of corporate prayer to close out your time as a group.

Weekly Leader Tips

- Remind students about the personal devotions and to complete Session 8 devotions as they conclude the study.

- Encourage students to memorize Session 8 memory verse this week.

- Challenge students to be in the habit of building into their own personal prayer lives what they have learned this week.

SOURCES

SESSION 3

1. Kendra Cherry, "What is a Genius IQ Score?," VeryWell Mind, accessed February 1, 2019, https://www.verywellmind.com/what-is-a-genius-iq-score-2795585.

2. "Christian Persecution Today," Open Doors USA, accessed February 1, 2019, https://www.opendoorsusa.org/christian-persecution/.

SESSION 5

1. Nissan Mindel, "The Three Daily Prayers," Kehot Publication Society, accessed February 1, 2019, https://www.chabad.org/library/article_cdo/aid/682091/jewish/The-Three-Daily-Prayers.htm.

2. "Strong's Concordance 3389. Yerushalaim or Yerushalayim," Bible Hub, accessed February 1, 2019, https://biblehub.com/hebrew/3389.htm.

SESSION 6

1. "StageofLife.com Trend Report: Teens Overcoming Fear," Stage of Life: Rewards for Life's Journey, accessed February 1, 2019, https://www.stageoflife.com/StageHighSchool/WhatDoTeensFear.aspx.

2. Pseudo-Clementine Homilies and Recognitions: (Justin, Apol. i. 26), and (Constt. Apost. ii. 14; 6:9), accessed February 1, 2019, http://www.earlychristianwritings.com/clementinerecognitions.html, http://www.earlychristianwritings.com/clementinehomilies.html.

3. Susanna Schrobsdorff, "Teen Depressesion and Anxiety: Why the Kids Are Not Alright," TIME magazine, Oct. 27. 2016, accessed February 1, 2019, http://time.com/magazine/us/4547305/november-7th-2016-vol-188-no-19-u-s/.

SESSION 7

1. "Test Anxiety." American Test Anxieties Assoication, accessed February 1, 2019, https://amtaa.org/.

2. "What is Hematidrosis?", WebMD, accessed February 1, 2019, https://www.webmd.com/a-to-z-guides/hematidrosis-hematohidrosis#1.

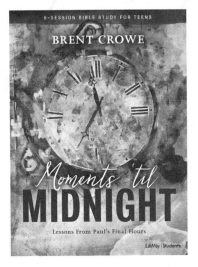
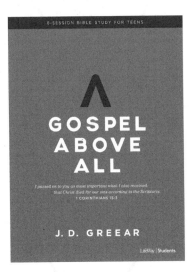
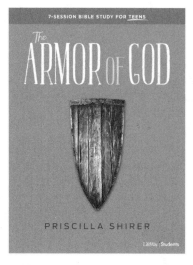